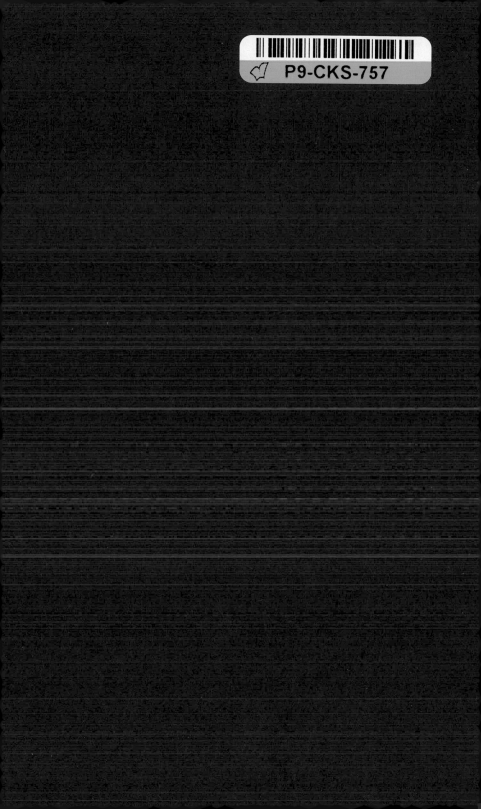

Different Seasons

Different Seasons

Twelve Months of

Wisdom & Inspiration

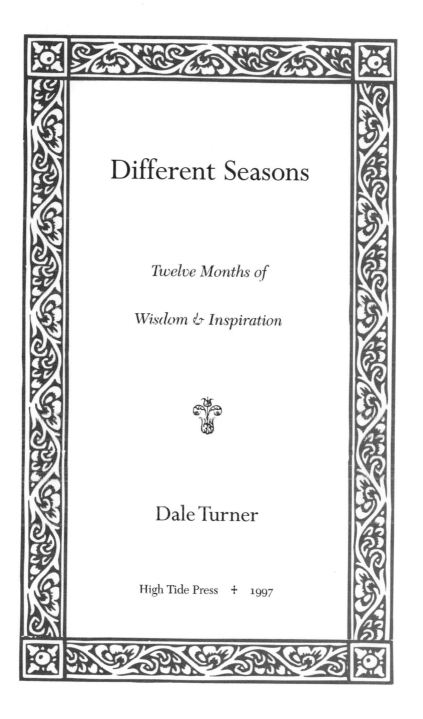

Dale Turner

High Tide Press   ✦   1997

A HIGH TIDE BOOK
Published by High Tide Press Inc.
1910 Ridge Road, Homewood, Illinois 60430

Library of Congress Catalog Card Number: 97-74991
Turner, Dale E. Different Seasons: Twelve months of
wisdom & inspiration / by Rev. Dale E. Turner – 1st ed.

ISBN 0-9653744-4-0

Book design by Alex Lubertozzi

Printed in the United States of America

First Edition

∞

The paper used in this publication meets the minimum
requirements of the American National Standard for
Information Sciences—Permanence of Paper for Printed
Library Materials, ANSI Z39.48-1984.

To my wife, Leone,
who edited and typed
columns for publication,
In Memory of our son,
Robert,
And with deepest gratitude
to Ruth Williamson-Kirkland
who worked countless hours
in preparing the columns
for this book.

He has told you, O mortal, what is good;
And what does the Lord require of you
but to do justice, and to love kindness,
and to walk humbly with your God?

Micah 6:8

Contents

Foreword

by Alex MacLeod

I WAS ABOUT twelve years old when I first met Dale Turner. I was a rambunctious, strong-willed kid, with more energy than good sense, the kind of boy only a mother could love—and then only on my very good days.

The year was 1958. The place was Seattle's University Congregational Church, where Dale had arrived to minister. I spent most Sunday mornings at U-Cong, as locals called it, in the company of my mother, father, brother, and three sisters.

Like in many churches, the services began with a hymn, a short, inspiring prayer, and a brief sermonette, aimed primarily at the children. After it was over, we kids raced off to Sunday School classes—called "character school" at U-Cong—leaving the adults behind for more hymns, prayers, and a full-blown, twenty-minute sermon.

Character school and I weren't meant for each other; I was just too devilish. Eventually, I was expelled back to the custody of my parents, forced to sit through the entire Sunday church service. And that was how I first came to know the truly wondrous talents of Dale Emerson Turner.

That's not to say Dale's sermonettes were shabby; they

weren't. They were regularly laced with humor and stories a kid could understand. Even better as far as I was concerned, they often featured athletes, many competing against the University of Washington, most coached by friends of Dale.

But good as they were, Dale's sermonettes couldn't hold a candle to his sermons, which helped fill the U-Cong's pews twice each Sunday for twenty-four years. What made his sermons so special was the clarity of his thought, the care of delivery, and the frequent touches of humor which only underscored the seriousness of his convictions. Dale obviously agreed with Oscar Wilde, who believed that "the only sin is that we take ourselves too seriously."

Dale's humor made me laugh, and his finely crafted messages made me think. It wasn't long before I felt lucky to have been kicked out of character school. This was something special.

By the time Dale retired from the pulpit, I had become a newspaper editor, having followed in my father's footsteps. My dad was happily retired himself, but still had a strong interest in *The Seattle Times*, where he'd worked for forty-three years.

"You know," he said, "I'll bet Dale could be a pretty good columnist. You might see if he'd be interested." I did, he was, and the rest—now nearly fifteen years—is, as they say, history. Let the record here show that probably the smartest idea I've had as an editor actually was my dad's.

Dale's weekly columns on our Saturday Religion page have been every bit as thoughtful—and popular—as his sermons. When he started, however, they were also just about as long.

I was Dale's first editor at *The Times*. His inaugural column was about our need for appreciation. It was written just like a sermon, and it took about twenty minutes to read. Editing it brought to mind a poem I'd heard from Dale years before:

> *When you get a thought that's happy,*
> *Boil it down.*
> *Make it short and crisp and snappy,*
> *Boil it down.*
> *When your brain its coin has minted,*
> *And down the page your pen has sprinted,*
> *If you want your effort printed,*
> *Boil it down.*

I reminded Dale of that poem, and that's about all it took for him to make the transition from preacher to newspaper columnist. His columns quickly attracted a large and loyal following. Not everyone agreed with everything he wrote—in fact, the courage of Dale's convictions on some key issues sparked strong dissent—but he became one of the best-read features in the newspaper, uncommon if not unprecedented among religion columnists.

Over the years, we have published hundreds of Dale Turner columns and republished many in a series of booklets. The booklets fly out the door as quickly as we print them. Requests come from all over the world. Usually, people ask for several copies to pass along to family and friends. Hardly a week goes by that I don't get a letter expressing thanks for Dale's columns.

In fact, the day I sat down to write this introduction I received a copy of a letter to Dale from a Seattle physician.

Attached was a note of thanks for running Dale's columns. Here's how his letter to Dale ended:

> Your thoughts have been an inspiration to me for many years and I just want you to know how much one soul does appreciate your continued guidance for our spiritual life.

I feel the same sense of gratitude. Among the many blessings in my life has been my long association with Dale Turner. This volume, which collects some of Dale's best columns, is a reminder of the wisdom and inspiration that have helped make our lives richer and better.

At the start of his ministry in 1943, Dale adopted a prayer to guide him:

> *Give me a sense of humor, Lord.*
> *Give me the grace to see a joke,*
> *To get some pleasure out of life*
> *And pass it on to other folk.*
> *Give me sympathy and sense*
> *And help keep my courage high.*
> *Give me calm and confidence,*
> *And, please, a twinkle in my eye.*

It is obviously a prayer fulfilled, both in his life and in these columns.

Managing Editor
The Seattle Times

Preface

THE COLUMNS COLLECTED here represent a portion of my ministry since my retirement as Senior Pastor of the University Congregational Church in Seattle. Since 1983 I have enjoyed the challenge of writing a weekly column for the Religion page at *The Seattle Times*.

A quick round with the calculator suggests—at fifty-two weekly articles times fifteen years—that I have written 780 articles. What a surprise to be confronted with one's own eventually prolific writing, all through a straightforward dedication to one's weekly task! This book, of roughly sixty selections, contains a representation of this year-in, year-out cycle, my relationship with my readers, and my reactions to my own life and the lives of my family, my friends, the community, and the world.

Each different season brings the opportunity to share ideas, thoughts, and questions common to us all. We all experience the particular joys and burdens of the winter holidays and new year, the patience and forbearance needed to see us through to the grateful rush of spring, of green and sunlight. Easter, Memorial Day, graduation, the Fourth of July, and summer vacation come and go in procession. The soft golden glow of the autumn sun, a brisk breeze, and the crisp falling leaves return, and we are again reminded of our thankfulness for the good that is ours.

There are also the times in our lives in which we may feel alone and yet we each share much of the experience in common; births, deaths, and marriages; the challenges of doubts, disabilities, disappointments, and sorrows. We all have questions about the meaning of life and the mysteries of God.

Writing my weekly column has given me the opportunity to share insights, inspirations, suggestions, and my own questions in a cycle of continual wonder, gratefulness, and joy. Each theme with it sorrows and joys is woven into the wheel of every circling year. Life has many spokes, but God is the hub. When all our activities and loyalties are rooted in God, life has unity, centrality, singleness of aim. It is our faith in and commitment to God that makes our lives whole and connects all the different seasons, the different nations, and different people.

My wife Leone has often said that I dig deeply into the big issues of life and theology and come up with simple truths. We can never be sure what effect our lives have on the lives of others, but I am hopeful that some of these simple truths will be of inspiration to you and will affect the good that you do each day, season upon changing season.

Dale E. Turner
Seattle, Washington
September 1997

Different Seasons

JANUARY

Each Day a Gift

N ITALY, BETWEEN Padua and Ferraro, is a villa with 365 windows. That's plenty of windows even in a large house—but some people say the original builder had the 365 days of the year in mind when he installed the windows. Perhaps the builder was suggesting that one could, and should, look upon the world each day from a different window.

This suggests an exciting philosophy to live by each day of the year.

It will rescue us from boredom, to say the least. Each day does bring its own unique gifts. It remains for us to untie the ribbons and accept the offerings as they appear.

An intelligent response to life is to find something positive in each new day. Unfortunately, many people simply endure the present and wait for a better time in the future. Today is always commonplace; it is yesterday that is beautiful and tomorrow that is full of possibilities.

Many young people gall under the restraints and disciplines of home and school, and yearn for the day when they can make their own decisions. Business men and women often look upon the present job as an undeserved interlude, waiting for the truly big opportunity to come. Parents simply endure the problems of rearing a family, as they dream of a time when budget and schedule will be less strained. How easily the present is disdained and its gifts unopened.

When we learn that each moment is alive with eternal issues, then, in some measure at least, we come to share the prerogative of a timeless God. Those who live nobly and receptively to God's continuing gifts know how to redeem each present hour.

But we are not merely the recipients of each day's gifts. We can determine in large measure what we shall put into the day. It is like filling our own stocking. For it is seldom true that we do not have a choice.

We are inclined to smile when we speak of New Year's resolutions; we know they are more easily made than kept. Yet those who have no conscious goals end up victims of the whims of chance. "No wind is favorable to one who does not know into which port he is trying to sail."

So why not consider goals that are worthy in the days ahead, and as you do:

- Begin each day with the affirmation found in Psalms 118:24: "This is the day that the Lord has made; let us rejoice and be glad in it."
- Give priority to essential concerns. Learn to distinguish what is more important from what is less important without making what is less important unimportant.
- Avoid procrastination. Do the thing you have to do when you have to do it, whether you feel like it or not.

* Learn to pause occasionally, or nothing worthwhile will catch up with you.
* Do one thing at a time and be all there when you do it. On Toscanini's eightieth birthday, someone asked his son, Walter, what his father considered his most important achievement. The reply was, "For him there can be no such thing. Whatever he happens to be doing at the moment is the biggest thing in his life—whether it is conducting a symphony or peeling an orange."
* Do something for someone else each day at some cost to yourself. More and more, I am convinced that the waste of life lies in the love we have not given and the powers we have not used. The selfish prudence that risks nothing and attempts to avoid pain misses happiness as well.

You may also wish to take seriously the advice offered by W. E. Channing, a well-known Unitarian minister: "To live content with small means; to seek elegance rather than luxury, and refinement rather than fashion; to be worthy, not respectable, and wealthy, not rich; to study hard, think quietly, talk gently, act frankly; to listen to stars and birds, to babes and sages, with open heart; to bear all cheerfully, to do all bravely, await occasions, hurry never.

"In a word, to let the spiritual, unbidden, and unconscious, grow up through the common."

❧

Bridge Builders & Peace Makers

IFE HAS CHANGED in countless ways since my boyhood days. The manner of road and bridge construction is but one.

When I was a boy, the road was built before the bridge. When a road came to a river or a gorge and it was necessary to build a span across, builders went to work.

Now when we drive through the country, we see big new bridges sitting out on the flats or crossing rivers with no roads at either end. They are the result of a master plan that calls for bridges first, and roads later. Once the bridges are built, we are committed to building a road.

For better or for worse, this is the way we operate in many areas of life. We make a down payment on a home and it is a bridge dictating a twenty- or thirty-year road of monthly payments.

Churches and businesses add people to their staffs because work needs to be done. The financial resources may not be in hand, but leaders force themselves to find more revenue because they believe in the ends they are trying to serve. They build the bridges first, trusting that roads will follow.

Today, deep crevasses separate nations. These must be bridged before roads can follow.

President Clinton went to Europe working to build bridges of understanding and cooperation for the mutual concern of the United States and European nations. It is good, right, and necessary that we remain involved beyond our own national borders.

It is significant that, at this time when our president is working to build bridges in Europe, we in the United States will be celebrating the birthday of the Rev. Dr. Martin Luther King Jr., one of the master bridge builders of our nation.

Dr. King said, "We are caught in an inescapable network of mutuality tied in a single garment of destiny. Whatever affects one directly affects all indirectly. We must be unrelenting in our quest for peace. The human family was not created to spiral down a militaristic stairway to a hell of nuclear destruction."

Despite many positive responses to Dr. King's call for justice, injustice and racial discrimination still persist. Millions of people are victims of discriminatory practices and policies, being denied their human rights because of their ethnic and social origin.

Prejudice builds walls of separation that are contrary to God's intent. We were created for community, and our lives have meaning as we relate to one another.

Anyone who breaks down walls of prejudice and alienation and builds bridges to unify is a great benefactor.

The Rev. Dr. Martin Luther King Jr. was such a man. This is one reason we rejoice that a national holiday observes his birth. January 15 means more than a time of school and office closures. It is a call to reflect on who Dr. King was, what he said, and what he did.

Like all great personalities, Dr. King did not want to be idolized but wanted his cause of unconditional love and nonviolence supported. The finest tribute we can pay to him is to free ourselves of prejudice, to work for peace and justice, to live with a consciousness of kinship with all people, and to accept responsibility for generations yet to come to do the same.

King, who idolized Gandhi and studied his life thoroughly, has been called the American Gandhi. Both Gandhi and King exemplified Jesus' teaching of turning the other cheek and going the second mile. Without pomp or pageantry, they proclaimed the centrality of unconditional love and nonviolence in human relations.

A study of King's life underlines the importance of early years and family life in shaping a child's career. It was in the presence of a strong mother and father that Martin's desire to fight against racial prejudice was kindled.

In his book *Stride Toward Freedom*, King tells of riding with his father when he accidentally drove past a stop sign: "A policeman pulled up to the car and said, 'All right, boy, pull over and let me see your license.' My father replied indignantly, 'I'm no boy.' Then pointing to me, he said, 'This is my boy. I am a man, and until you call me one, I will not listen to you.' The policeman was so shocked that he wrote the ticket up nervously, and left the scene as quickly as possible."

That experience was one of many that deepened in young Martin the determination to devote his life to justice and equality so that blacks would not experience humiliation or be relegated to the status of second-class citizens.

Dr. King would have been the last person to claim himself free of flaws. Like all humans, he had imperfections, yet far overarching any fallibilities was his deep faith and total commitment to everything just, fair, and loving. He was courageous and willing to pay whatever price was required to share his message of unconditional love and nonviolence.

Without hope for praise or fear of blame, he openly identified himself with the cause of racial justice and equality for all people. Death threats came often, yet he did not soften his call for justice. He said, "If physical death is the price that I must pay to free my white brothers and sisters from a permanent death of the spirit, then nothing can be more redemptive."

Dr. King was a graphic writer and an eloquent speaker. He spoke truths in a way that enabled them to remain in the mind of the listener or reader. I have kept a file of his comments that I have wanted to retain, for they are worth pondering and applying to everyday life:

> Any religion that has no concern about the social and economic conditions that scar the soul is a spiritually moribund religion, only waiting for the day to be buried. A religion that ends with the individual, ends.

> Nonviolence is a powerful and just weapon ... which cuts without wounding and ennobles the man who wields it. It is a sword that heals.

> A riot is the language of the unheard.

> I believe that unarmed truth and unconditional love will

have the final word in reality. This is why right, temporarily defeated, is stronger than evil triumphant.

I never knew Dr. King, but I did have the privilege of meeting him in 1961 when he visited Seattle. I also spoke with him briefly at Chicago's O'Hare airport a few weeks before he was assassinated in 1968. Although he is not alive to visit us again, his words live on to challenge and inspire us.

I am reminded of the words of a humble poem, memorized and recited by many in days gone by, that deserves to be resurrected, not for the elegance of its rhyme but for the counsel it conveys:

An old man, going a lone highway,
Came at evening, cold and gray,
To a chasm, vast and deep and wide,
Through which was flowing a sullen tide.
The old man crossed in the twilight dim,
The sullen stream had no fears for him,
But he turned when safe on the other side
And built a bridge to span the tide.

"Old man," said a fellow pilgrim near,
"You're wasting your strength with building here;
Your journey will end with the ending day;
You never again must pass this way;
You have crossed the chasm, deep and wide,
Why build you the bridge at eventide?"

The builder lifted his old gray head:
"Good friend, in the path I have come," he said,
"There followeth after me today

A youth whose feet must pass this way.
This chasm that has been naught to me
To that fair-haired youth may a pitfall be.
He, too, must cross in the twilight dim;
Good friend, I am building the bridge for him."

—Will Allen Dromgoole

This article originally appeared on January 15, 1994 in
The Seattle Times, *with additional material from January 16, 1993.*

Life Ephemeral

A s WE TURN the pages of the world's literature, more than once we come across sad, impressive words permeated with a sense of the brevity of our days upon earth.

An old Anglo-Saxon writer compares life to a little bird that flies in through a window, flutters around for a few brief moments, and then wings its way out.

And it is one of Homer's characters who says: "Even as are the generations of leaves, such are those likewise of men; the leaves that be the wind scattereth on the earth, and the forest buddeth and putteth forth more again, when the season of spring is at hand; so of the generations of men; one putteth forth and another ceaseth."

But such words are to most of us little more than rhetoric until we have lived long enough to witness for ourselves the drama of the passing generations. When we see those whom we knew as little children bearing the burden of manhood and womanhood and rearing their own families; when others whom we have thought of as vigorous in middle life grow bent and gray; when hairs disappear from our own heads, and facial wrinkles appear; and we see carved in memorial granite the names of our neighbors of just yesterday; then we know what our forebears meant when they sang: "Our days are as the grass or like the morning flower."

A contemporary writer, Adelaide Crapsey, asks:

Why have
I thought the dew
Ephemeral when I
Shall rest so short a time, myself,
On earth?

Several fall seasons ago, I traveled across West Virginia, the state of my birth, to attend a reunion of our college football team in Buckhannon, West Virginia. The journey to the reunion was a memorable one. I saw again the tree-covered hills and mountain streams I had come to love when I was a youngster.

Along the roadside stood the old ivy-mantled homesteads and the big stone barns, looking not very different from what they did as I traveled their way many years before. The hills wore again the many-tinted glory of autumn. Corridors of color were everywhere to be seen. The brown fields joined each to each as in days gone by. The broad road still wound over the hill and through the valley, but those who once traveled it are gone. Another generation treads the paths worn by the feet of their fathers and mothers.

It is not a morbid thought that I express. It is simply descriptive of the way our lives are lived. Our days are as the shadow that flies across the sunny hill, as the flower that blossoms and fades. The years pass more swiftly than a weaver's shuttle. Joseph Cook put it all in one short sentence: "Striving twenties; thriving thirties; fiery forties; faithful fifties; sober sixties; solemn seventies; aching eighties; the sod; God!"

But the swift passing of years is a call to give priority to values of worth in the brief days allotted to us. It is possible in this life to major in minors—to spend the majority of our time doing that which is of little importance. It is recorded of one of the princes of France that his principal occupation was killing weasels in barns. There are plenty of weasel-killers in the world. It is easy to develop the habit of wasting hour after hour in trivialities while life races speedily by.

A shorter working day means more leisure, but an abundance of leisure is for some a doubtful blessing, and for others an absolute curse. Thousands of people in America today have ample time to make their lives count in their communities. Great books remain unread, letters are left unwritten, calls unmade, and acts of love and kindness are neglected and left undone.

There is no satisfaction for self or others in such idleness. The prayer of the psalmist is relevant in any age: "So teach us to number our days that we may apply our hearts unto wisdom." In his fine book, *Peace of Mind*, Rabbi Josh Liebman reminds us that, "Death is not the enemy of life, but its friend, for it is the knowledge that our years are limited which makes them so precious."

The presence of death makes more meaningful all of the values of life. It is the truth that time is but lent to us which makes us give our best, looking upon our years as a trust handed into our temporary keeping. While we live, we should try to make each day count, as far as beauty, nobility, and a warm sense of brotherhood are concerned. In a time when there is so much cruelty in our world, we must generate the oxygen of love to keep the soul of the world still breathing.

We are called to deepen the quality of life as a compensation for the diminution of its quantity, to treasure each other in the recognition that we do not know how long we shall have each other, and to make life strong and brave and beautiful with acts of kindness and caring while it is yet day.

☙

Little Things

E ARE LIVING in an age obsessed by bigness and size. We are easily impressed by big cities, tall buildings, and large corporations. We look at enrollment figures as a guide to the greatness of schools and universities. We sometimes read from the book of numbers to determine the vitality of a church.

One man, speaking despairingly, said we are afflicted with the disease of "Jumboism."

To stress the big, stupendous, or colossal can be unfortunate, not because they are insignificant, but because we miss more important aspects of life.

Often many influential factors of life are small, obscure, and inconspicuous. Although small, they have power to heal or to harm.

Many in our community and across the country are very aware of that right now. A little flu bug, unseen to the naked eye, has been knocking big people off their feet.

Fortunately, there are also microbes within the body that are sentinels, protecting against illness. Consider the white corpuscles of the blood—so small they can be seen only with powerful microscopes, yet they are the body's greatest health agents.

Like little detectives, they pounce upon bits of poison and carry them from the body. How easy it is to remain unaware of the life-giving powers within our bodies because they are invisible and diminutive.

Just as we can overlook much of importance going on inside the body, it is possible to be blind to important events in society because they seem inconsequential in the presence of "big" news.

Had we been reporters in Palestine at the time of the birth of Jesus, we would have written much about Herod's rule, the Roman legion, and Pilate's court. Such pageantry, glamour, and grandeur seemed the real news of the day.

It remained for wise men to see the humble, obscure birth of a baby as a revolutionizing force of life.

What sentimentalists, some might say, to worship a baby! Sentimentalists, perhaps, but realists, too. For Herod, Pilate, and Rome's glory are gone, but Jesus is living still.

Had we been reporters in 1809, what would have been the big news? Surely we would have reported Napoleon's march across Europe with war and destruction. Those stories would have been the great news of the day! How difficult it would have been to have seen the importance of a few birth announcements—but Cyrus McCormick, Charles Darwin, William Gladstone, Abraham Lincoln, Oliver Wendell Holmes, Edgar Allen Poe, and Alfred, Lord Tennyson have made that year famous.

The great seers of life have not been fooled by size or numbers. William James, one of America's great thinkers, saw the fallacy of believing in size or greatness alone.

He said, "As for me, my bed is made. I am against *big-ness* and *greatness* in all their forms and with the invisible, molecular, moral forces that work from individual to individual *stealing* in through the crannies of the world like as many soft rootlets, or like the capillary oozing of water, yet rending the hardest monuments of men's pride, if you give them time."

In my library is a book written by C. S. Lewis. Published in 1943, it continues to stay in print. The book, *The Screwtape Letters*, is a series of letters written from hell by Screwtape, ruler of the lowerarchy, to his nephew, Wormwood, who is working here on Earth. Wormwood is a novice tempter who is trying to win people to hell and is discouraged because his client has committed no big crimes and is moving too slowly in that direction.

Screwtape, wiser than his young nephew, writes to him:

> You say he is committing only very small sins. But like every young tempter you are anxious to report more spectacular wickedness. It does not matter how small the sins are provided their cumulative effect is to edge men away from the light out into the nothing. Murder is no better than cards if cards can do the trick. Indeed, the safest road to hell is the gradual one, the gentle slope, soft underfoot, without sudden turning, without milestones, without signposts.

Screwtape understood that it is the little evils that lay waste a life. As a rule, we do not lose our integrity and honor by a blowout. It is usually a small leak—a transgression here, a neglect there, until, without the clanking of chains, evil has us bound.

The good life, too, is the compilation of many "littles"—acts of honor, kindness, thoughtfulness, and love. Similes used by Jesus show his appreciation of little things.

He spoke of the mustard seed, proverbially. Although not actually the smallest seed, it can become a great tree, large enough for birds to nest in its branches. "If you have faith," said Jesus, "even as a grain of mustard seed, nothing is impossible unto you." He also spoke of leaven. Although used in small amounts, it is quantitatively active, permeating a large lump of dough.

He told his followers they were the salt of the Earth. Salt is also microscopically small when compared with its potent and vital uses. Salt, in Jesus' day, as today, was used to preserve and add flavor to food. It was also often added to candles or lamps to give sparkle or luster to the flame.

Jesus' followers were to be like salt, not ostentatious and dramatic but quietly preserving the highest ideas and ideals, adding radiance and luster to life.

Sometimes when I consider the tremendous consequences that follow from little things—a chance word, a letter, a call, a tap on the shoulder—I am tempted to think there are no little things. For a life can be made or broken by such as these—little things.

❧

Deliberate Acts of Kindness

HEN KING EDWARD VII of England was Prince of Wales, he hosted a formal dinner to honor a man for many distinguished achievements. The table etiquette of the guest had not kept pace with his rise to fame, and when the tea was served, he poured some of it into his saucer to cool before drinking it. Looks of mild surprise and some suppressed smiles went around the table.

Taking in the situation at once, the prince immediately poured some of his tea into his saucer and began to drink from it. Several of the guests saw the gesture and did likewise. For that particular occasion, drinking from one's saucer became royal table etiquette.

Saving a guest of honor from embarrassment was a kingly act on the part of the prince. And whether the story is apocryphal or true, it is an object lesson in kindness.

In his booklet, "The Power of Kindness," Harry M. Tippett calls kindness "the loveliest flower in the garden of virtue. It blooms in every kind of soil, and often in the darkest corners. It knows no particular season, and it flourishes in every latitude." Kindness is, indeed, needed in our world today. All can use its renewing and encouraging power.

Outward appearances are often deceiving. A smiling person may be nursing a deep hurt. There are lots of good actors around—those capable of appearing carefree while their souls are in anguish. Be kind. The milk of human kindness nourishes both body and soul. Kindness expresses itself in many ways. It may be an understanding smile for a friend. It may be a phone call, a card or a letter. It may be a visit, or a staying away when another person wants or needs to be alone. It may be quiet, empathetic listening.

Kindness may express itself in putting the baby bird back in the nest or in putting the broken bottle into a trash can. It may be in letting another have the biggest piece of candy or the last cookie. It may be in not asking what it is when a child shows us his drawing.

Kindness may come in the form of a reprimand. Mrs. Harvey Bisbee was a colleague of mine in Michigan. I will always remember her as a devoted church worker, but I will remember her more especially for her wisdom as a mother.

She did a kindness to the older of her two sons by reprimanding him and denying him privileges because he returned from a long hike leaving his younger brother so far behind that he became tearful and afraid.

Gordon, that older son, has never forgotten her wisdom. He traces the concern he has now for those who lag behind in education or finance to the insight that came to him from his mother in the act of kindness that took the form of censure. How valuable it is when business and professional men and women see kindness as relevant in the work that they are doing.

The *Detroit Free Press* carried the story of Sam Reeve, who was invited a few years ago to a presidential White

House Conference on Small Business. Sam had started twenty years before with only a few dollars, and had multiplied them into one of the largest service-station businesses in the state of Michigan. The administration wanted to know how he had done it.

His place of business was not exclusive—the three other corners of the intersection had stations as large and bright, and carried comparable quality merchandise. "I just try to give away more than my competitors," Sam said. Give away stamps or prizes, or chances on new cars? No. Sam gives away service, acts of kindness, and caring.

After every snowstorm, he plows the snow from the driveways of those who need it. He baby-sits with youngsters, picks up grocery orders, meets unexpected guests at the airport, checks the heat or lights in the homes of customers while they are on vacation. And he never charges a dime!

When someone asked him where he got the idea, Sam pointed to a dog-eared, scotch-taped Bible, "It belonged to my dad," he said, "and I try to run the station by this passage: 'Give and it shall be given unto you; good measure pressed down, and shaken together, and running over ... for with the same measure that ye mete withal it shall be measured to you again!'" (Luke 6:38)

His countless kindnesses won for Sam Reeve not only a host of friends, but also grateful customers and a profitable business. And he had the time of his life when he saw the joy he was bringing to others.

Kindness also has great transforming power. When Eugene Debs was imprisoned as a conscientious objector during World War I, he became interested in a black prisoner who was said to be incorrigible, lacking even a spark of goodness. Since the black man would not speak to anyone, Debs started a campaign of kindness by leaving an orange on the black man's bed and going off without a word. Despite many rebuffs, he gradually penetrated the hard exterior of the man, and the two became friends.

Years later, at the news of Debs' death, the black man, now a useful citizen, said, "He was the only Jesus Christ I ever knew."

Stephen Greliet, a French born Quaker who lived in America, would be unknown in the world today except for a few lines that make him immortal. When carried in the heart, they can direct us all:

"I shall pass through this world but once. Any good therefore that I can do, or any kindness that I can show to any human being, let me do it now. Let me not defer or neglect it, for I shall not pass this way again."

FEBRUARY

A Concise Sermon

READ A NEWS report with a photo of the Reverend John Albrecht, an Episcopal priest who entered the *Guinness Book of World Records* by standing before his Lake Orion, Michigan, congregation and giving the shortest sermon on record.

He stood and uttered one word: "Love." Then he sat down. That was it. No more.

One of his members said it was his best sermon. Certainly it must have taken some time to prepare. I have long been told that, "Church would be nicer if sermons were conciser."

Actually, I'm envious of John Albrecht's innovative spirit. I've been pondering how to come up with a one-word sermon to tie his record. I might try words such as care, gift, lift, help, kind, or Lord. The possibilities are limitless. Or I might try to better his record with a two-letter word—be, me, go, or up. Better yet, a combination of two-letter words—"If it is to be, it is up to me."

I suspect that any congregation where I might preach would welcome that effort, more than a try at the record for the world's longest sermon—sixty hours and thirty-one minutes, by a Unitarian minister.

Public speakers are taught that it is better to drive home one point than to leave three stranded on bases. Certainly the Reverend Mr. Albrecht did that to the *n*th degree. His word—love—has never lacked for testimonials, but it also has its detractors.

Julian Huxley wrote an indictment of the word: "Of all the worn, smudged, dog-eared words in our vocabulary, surely love is the grubbiest, smelliest, slimiest. Bawled from a million pulpits, it becomes an outrage to good feeling and decent taste, an obscenity that one hates to pronounce."

I can understand his disgruntlement. The word love is so abused, and in such varied contexts, that its deeper meanings are caricatured, distorted, or missed entirely. Ads tell us that love is running together through a meadow, lighting two cigarettes in the dark, or applying a deodorant daily. We are given the idea that love "just happens" and usually at first sight. You don't have to work at love, it requires no teacher, no special responses, no disciplines. You simply "fall into love." This is sheer nonsense.

Admittedly love is not easy to define. How do we rationalize a mystery? How do we capture the waves of the sea in a fishing net, or imprison love in a web of words?

Can we pin love down like a specimen butterfly in a showcase, dissect its wings, or discover its beauty? Some things defy complete analysis or definition—yet, even so, are reasonably clear.

Love is more than a feeling. It is determined, undiscourageable goodwill. Love is justice distributed; it is friendship set to music, caring crystallized and expressed in specific acts and attitudes toward self and others.

Love is not blind. It sees clearly: it sees beyond what is to the good that yet may be. It sees beneath the soil to the seed of possibility.

Love does not dominate. It cultivates. It encourages. Love knows there is lovability in each person, even if undiscovered.

Love is the active power enabling us to break through walls that separate us from others. It is the doorway through which the human spirit moves from solitude to society, from selfishness to service. Love permits us to overcome our isolation and separateness, and yet, permits us to be ourselves.

"Sometime," wrote Pierre Teilhard de Chardin, "after mastering the winds, the waves, the tides and gravity, we shall harness for God the energies of love—and then for the second time in the history of the world, man will discover fire."

John Albrecht, you knew what you were doing. It was theatrics, gimmickry, or a desire to break into *Guinness* that inspired you to do what you did. It was an ingenious way of setting before us the one word above all others that captures the essence of all great religions. Bless you for it.

❧

Adversity Can Help, Too

HE STORY IS told of a young Persian prince about to ascend the throne. Acutely aware of his need for more knowledge and wisdom, he called his court philosophers and wise men and commanded them to prepare a history of humankind. They began at once.

Twenty years later, they presented the king with the fruits of their research—six thousand volumes. Too busy at that time with the affairs of state to read that many books, the king ordered his wise men to condense their findings into one book. Another twenty years passed, and at last the wise men presented the king with the book he had asked for.

But the king was now far too old and sick to read the book. From his death bed the king looked up at his wise men and asked, "Then shall I die without knowing the history of humankind?"

"Sir," replied one of the wise men, "I will sum it up for you in seven words: they were born; they suffered; they died."

That seems far too grim and gloomy an appraisal, for life has much beauty and joy. Yet there is much suffering and sadness, too. There are countless misfortunes that all may encounter—or as Emerson said, "A crack in everything God has made."

Could it be that the crack, the problem, may turn out to be a blessing in disguise? Our response to disappointment, frustration, and thwarted hopes is conditioned in part by what we believe life to be. If we expect a trouble-free existence, then any interruption of our tranquillity is an intruder to be resented. But if we see trouble as an inevitable aspect of life, even as a prod to something finer, then it can be turned to constructive ends. When we begin by realizing that life is hard, it then can be easier for us.

The orientation we give our young is not often in this direction.

Keith Miller, in his fine book, *The Taste of New Wine*, says we train our children to be subtly dishonest almost from the crib. We train them to look happy and successful, to hide their true feelings and hurts and to appear better than they are or feel.

Because we are taught to do this, others do not share their inmost feeling with us, nor do we with them, so we assume that they are better off than they are.

No doubt there is truth in Miller's observation. Perhaps it would be refreshing if, when we asked another how he is, he would respond with, "How much time do you have?" "Do you really want to know?" "I feel terrible." "I am a walking hospital."

Would we ask that person how he was the next time we saw him?

I do not believe we are intentionally deceitful when we cover our grief or pain and respond to questions concerning our welfare with "great" or "fine."

In a sense, suffering is relative, and if we have a headache or a sore back, it isn't as bad as it would be if we were starving or critically ill—so, in a sense, we are "fine."

A big worry always drives out a smaller one. Perhaps that is why humanity survives so many threats. A man can sit in pain with an abscessed tooth and if someone yells "fire!" his mouth is well again and you have to remind him when the fire is out that he has a toothache.

The truth is we all hurt in one way or another. There are no trouble-free lives. Such knowledge prompts a sense of compassion in all caring people.

Happily, there are positive possibilities in the troubles we encounter. The characteristics that we most admire in human nature grow best in a soil mixed with trouble. Without hardship, there would be no hardihood. Without calamity there would be no courage. Without trouble there would be no triumphant living.

It is no mystery why the sixteenth president of our nation, Abraham Lincoln, inspires us all. His character and integrity were the result of his ability to handle and overcome adversity.

Born in the humblest of circumstances, he fought hard for privileges we now take for granted: education, democracy, equal opportunity. As a young lawyer in Springfield, Illinois, he ran for the legislature and was defeated.

Then he tried business and failed. When he fell in love with a young woman who finally loved him in return, she died. He spent one year in Congress in 1846, but was defeated for re-election. He failed to get an appointment to the U. S. Land Office, lost his bid for the U. S. Senate and for the vice presidential nomination.

When he finally became president, the country was torn asunder by the Civil War, which he would have given his life to prevent.

But he never hated anyone, never sought revenge, never lost touch with the common people, and never gave up.

Much as we deplore the adversities Lincoln suffered, we know that his quality of character never could have come from a life of ease, comfort and pleasantness alone. He did not simply endure in the midst of privation and disappointment—he prevailed.

❦

Grief Brings Healing

THERE IS ONE thing all people have in common. We all experience grief. Tennyson wrote, "Never morning wore to evening that some heart did not break." In a world where grief is ever present, it is wise to learn how to deal with it constructively.

We are introduced to grief early—a broken toy, the loss of a pet, a family move, or one of many other experiences. As we grow older, grief may come in the form of an unsuccessful marriage or no marriage at all. It may come with the loss of a job, the deterioration of health—or the loss of a child or spouse, the most agonizing of all.

Most people pass through several stages of grieving before healing comes. And it may be helpful to know that counselors specially trained in grief therapy are available.

The initial response at the time of sorrow is shock or disbelief. The shock provides insulation until the time comes when we can deal rationally with the new situation. For some, the stage lasts only a few minutes to a few hours. For others, it may last days or even weeks. It is wise to keep as busy as possible.

Eventually, shock merges into acceptance as full realization of the loss begins. Then it is normal and good that tears come. We have been given tear glands for a purpose and we should use them. Tears are a safety valve of the heart when too much pressure is laid upon it.

There are those who are inclined to apologize for their tears. "I am so weak," they say. Or, "I know I am being foolish to shed so many tears—where is my faith?" Tears are not signs of weakness, foolishness, or lack of faith. Tears are evidence of the capacity to care.

Those who hope to help one who is grieving must respect his pain and accept that tears are vital to his health. Suppressing tears actually hinders the process of working through loss.

Acknowledging and expressing pain helps the griever recover a sense of self and find renewal. One psychiatrist called tears "agony in solution." Tears help flush grief from the soul.

When a loved one dies, it is normal for the bereaved to go through a period of sharp questioning, guilt, and self-reproach. We often hear words like, "I wasn't sympathetic enough. Why didn't I show more love and gratitude while he was alive?" When suicide is involved, the self-condemnation is usually heightened, for we wonder if we could have done something. As a rule, we are harder on ourselves than the facts warrant.

Feelings of anger are often present in the midst of grief—anger at ourselves or others, or even anger directed toward the one who has left us. It is a human response, and we need to direct it in constructive ways.

When the tears have been shed, the guilt felt, and the anger expressed, it is normal to experience deep feelings of loneliness when it may seem that God doesn't care. One may even wonder if there is a God at all. It is common to feel depressed when someone or something treasured is taken away. Fortunately, continuous loneliness and depression do not need to persist.

Several years ago, I counseled a woman whose husband had been killed in an accident. Her deep grief seemed inconsolable. I suggested to her that the pain would never fully disappear, but the day would come when the fog and darkness would lift enough so that her despair over the loss of her husband would give way to gratitude for having had him for forty-two years of married life. Many months later, she said to me, "You were right. I find myself singing again."

In 1965, I called at the home of David and Lucile Bassett to visit with their twenty-year-old son, Don, who was dying of cancer. I went to his room and sat by his bed. Don was a very bright and creative person, and was cheerful even in pain.

"I do not know why this is happening to me," he said. "I love life and want to live, but if I can live no longer, I am grateful for the life I have had, for my wonderful parents, brothers and sister, and for all the friends that are mine. I'm not sure I know exactly how to handle this, for I have never died before, but I shall try to be brave, whatever comes."

Don and I joined hands and I offered a prayer. Then I returned to be with the family waiting outside.

We were silent for a very long time. I leaned against a wall and wept, and we all wept together. I remember feeling embarrassed after I left because I had not been able to control my emotions.

This past Christmas I received a letter from Bobbie,

Don's sister, who was a teenager at the time of Don's death. She said that my tears in their midst were the most moving and memorable experience of her life. Our friendship, which has deepened through the years, was solidified when we wept together.

Grief knits hearts in closer bonds than happiness can, and common sufferings are far stronger than common joys.

Silence Is Golden

OT EVERYONE WHO has the gift of speech understands the value of silence.

The sun goes forth each day to run its race but we never hear its panting or catch the sound of its footsteps. We do not hear its life-giving warmth. We do not hear the moon rise or set. The stars come up nightly without loud fanfares.

Positive things can happen when we are still, when we pause and reflect. But silence is hard to find in a huge, busy city.

This is an age and place of noise and speed. The air vibrates with the thunder of giant engines. Planes, trucks, and trains rumble and sirens pierce the calm.

We are continually immersed in a bath of noise. A juke box in a tavern in Brooklyn has one item entitled, "Five minutes of silence for a quarter." Understandably, it gets regular play.

At home, the TV, radio, and stereo dominate the scene. "Turn that thing down!" is the phrase that triggers more arguments in the home than any other. Parents sometimes wish that children could be controlled with knobs.

We empathize with the mother of three small boys who, when asked what she was going to do while her sons spent a week with grandparents, responded, "I'm going to do something I haven't done in years—listen to the silence."

Constant exposure to noise or sound is debilitating. It shatters nerves, detracts from vitality and shortens life. It could be one reason why physical, mental, and emotional breakdowns are increasing at an alarming pace, particularly in urban areas.

Geoffrey Fisher, an Archbishop of Canterbury, had a good observation about the value of silence. "In the cities no one is quiet, but many are lonely," he said. "In the country people are quiet, but few are lonely."

Happily, there are places where we can go to find refuge from the city's din. We can easily drive to places of spectacular beauty and inspiration—the Pacific and Atlantic coasts, the Smokey and Rocky Mountain ranges, the prairies of the Midwest, the rainforests of the Pacific Northwest, the bayous and beaches of the Southeast, the deserts of the Southwest, and the countless lakes, forests, canyons, and rivers of this great land.

I remember vividly the time my wife, Leone, and I drove to Crystal Mountain in mid-winter. We don't ski, but we took the lift to the top of the very highest mountain. It was a clear, crisp day. The sky was blue and was breathtakingly beautiful. A fresh blanket of snow covered the mountain.

Earth had nothing more fair to show. But most of all we were impressed by the silence. It was a living, breathing, speaking silence. The wind stirred and it was a mere sigh in the stately trees. The soft sound of a wheel on the wire lift merely emphasized the peace it disturbed. The silence was more eloquent than any human voice. There was a deeper beauty than any poem could adequately express and it throbbed with a secret too great to be told. It is in such a place of beauty that the heart finds its healing, the spirit its rest, and God's presence is made known.

In nature, only the destructive forces such as winds, explosions, storms, and thunder are noisy. The healing forces are silent. We do not hear the greening of the grass, the blossoming of the bush, the flowering of the shrub.

We do not hear the force of gravity holding us to earth. The seasons change in silence. We experience the peace of day, the sunset's glory, the grace of flowers. All are hallelujahs to the creator, and yet meaningless silences to those who have no ear.

If we were truly still, we would not think that God was still. Commotions that we make prevent God's voice from being heard. If we hush ourselves, we may awaken to his language, for God's good word sounds through the wind.

> *If you stand very still at a difficult hour and wait*
> *for a silence within,*
> *You will be led in wisdom and strength through a*
> *world of confusion and din.*
> *If year after year you keep inwardly still, God will*
> *give you the help that you ask.*
> *In the silence God gives you will find what you*
> *need—his wisdom, his strength for each task.*

Love Indefinable

T IS NOT surprising to learn that in a newspaper poll to determine the ten favorite words of Americans, the word "love" led all the rest by a wide margin. No word is more widely praised and yet more difficult to accurately and fully define.

Try as we will to define love it still eludes us. Shakespeare wrote 150 sonnets attempting to capture the essence of love and had to confess failure.

How can we rationalize a mystery? How do we capture the waves of the sea in a fishing net, or imprison love in a web of words? Can we pin love down like a specimen butterfly in a show case and say—there! No. Some things are so ethereal and continuously mysterious that they cannot be defined. They can more easily be demonstrated. William James, when asked to define "spiritual" responded, "I cannot define it, but I can point to one who embodies in his life all that the word means to me"—and he pointed to Phillips Brooks, the eminent clergyman and scholar.

It is when we see our love expressed in specific individuals and particular relationships that its deepest meanings begin to become clear. Most of us experienced love before we ever began to try to define it.

The older I grow, the more I marvel at the miracle which transformed my boyhood home. The miracle is that although we were poor, I never knew it, for poverty in things was obscured by a richness in love and caring that knew no limits. If there was nothing in our pockets, we four children always knew our buttons were intact and our shirts clean. Our parents' hearts overflowed with love which was never conditional or altered by circumstance. No infraction was so small that it was condoned nor was any failure so large it would not be forgiven.

The memory of my own childhood experience is one of the reasons it saddens me to hear a parent say of a son or daughter away at school, in the service, or living in another community, "I haven't heard from that child of mine in weeks, and I told her I wasn't going to write again until she wrote to me."

Sometimes we hear more serious threats, such as, "I told my son that if he made that choice [chose that lifestyle, married that girl], he needn't bother to come back to this house—ever!" Of course this is not love. It is bruised pride, a play for power, and a far cry from genuine love.

Thoughtful people who have been reared in loving homes always want to express their appreciation for the early training they have received, but many make the mistake of waiting too long to do this. The bitterest tears are often those shed at a gravesite when it is remembered that the words of the gratitude so long felt have never been spoken or written.

One man in his thirties, recalling the days of his childhood, wrote to his parents at Easter: "Thank you for hiding my Easter eggs in such a way that they were easy to find and for giving me so much love I never had to look for it." Such a letter cannot be seen as "sticky" sentimentality. Rather, it is evidence of maturity and a genuine sense of appreciation.

Unfortunately, intelligent and caring love is not present in all homes. Each day we are reminded in the press and on TV that the incidence of child abuse is escalating at an alarming rate. It is tragic for the children who are abused and for the future it foretells. Abusive adults are often those who were themselves abused when they were children.

As harmful and indefensible as physical abuse of children and young people is, it is sad that verbal abuse is often less censored or subject to a criminal charge, for negative words can hit as hard as a fist and leave deep and lasting scars. It is abusive to a child to destroy initiative and a sense of self-worth with such debilitating phrases as, "You are hopeless;" "You can never do anything right;" "You will never amount to anything;" "I can't wait till you grow up and get out of this house." Such biting and unkind comments are not spoken in homes where love undergirds and permeates family relationships.

I have long been impressed by the centrality Judaism gives to love in family life. Jewish teachings abound in detailing the responsibility family members have to love and care for each other.

A Jewish legend illustrates how beautiful family love and caring can be: Two brothers lived on adjoining farms— one was married and the other, a bachelor. Their farms were of equal size, and at the harvest one farm was seen to be just as fruitful as the other. The wheat had been cut and was standing in sheaves in the fields.

The married brother, sitting in his home and thinking of his bachelor brother, said, "He is a lonely man. He has no wife, no children, no joy in his life except what he buys. I think I will take some of my sheaves and put them in his field tonight."

It so happened that the bachelor was thinking of the married brother with his wife and children, and he said, "Brother has many mouths to feed and I don't need all I have. I'll take some of my sheaves and put them in his field tonight."

Secretly carrying out their plans, they met face to face one dark night. Learning of each other's act of love and caring, they embraced tearfully and expressed gratitude for the love that bound them together. The legend says that at the spot where they met, the Temple was built, for there, heaven was nearest to earth.

Martin Buber, the Jewish religious scholar and philosopher, said, "Those who love bring God and the world together."

MARCH

We All Need to Be Appreciated

EVERAL DAYS AGO I discovered in my files the record of a charming note written by William James to the members of his philosophy class at Radcliffe College. Professor James had been ill, and his students had sent him an azalea plant and their best wishes for a speedy recovery.

"I am deeply touched by your remembrance," he wrote in a note of thanks. "It is the first time anyone ever treated me so kindly, so you may well believe that the impression on the heart of the lonely sufferer will be even more durable than the impression on your mind of all the teachings of Philosophy 2-A.

"I now perceive one immense omission in my psychology. The deepest principle of human nature is the craving to be appreciated, and I left it out altogether from the book because I have never had it gratified till now.

"I fear you have let loose a demon in me, and that all my actions will now be for the sake of such rewards. Believe in the extreme pleasure you have caused me, and in the affectionate feeling with which I am, and shall always be, faithfully, your friend, William James."

This most gracious note, with the felicitous phrases of another generation, is quite touching. Here was one of our nation's greatest philosophers, confessing with not a little poignancy that his "craving to be appreciated" had never been gratified in such a way before.

If we honestly search our own hearts, I believe we will clearly recognize two truths in our own lives that confirm what William James wrote to his philosophy class.

First, nothing lifts us up and sets us moving toward greater accomplishments than the simple word or gesture of appreciation for that which we already have done. I don't think we should make any apology in declaring this need for ourselves. James was right when he said, "The deepest principle of human nature is the craving to be appreciated."

Second, the sad truth is that we have not always expressed genuine appreciation as often, or as fully, as we should. This thought gives me a measure of pain, and I wonder if it is not so with you. The hurried to-and-fro nature of our time has been too much in command and the simple—but sincere—expressions of gratitude and affection too long delayed.

There is a maxim to which we all wisely might subscribe: "You can never do a kindness too soon for you never know how soon it will be too late."

❧

Up from the Ashes

HEN ROBINSON CRUSOE was wrecked on his lonely isle, he drew up in two columns what he called the evil and the good:

He was cast on a desert island, but was still alive, not drowned as all his ship's company were. He was divided from humankind, but he was not starving. He had no clothes, but he was in a hot climate where he didn't need them. He was without defense, but he saw no wild beasts.

He concluded that no condition in the world was so miserable that there wasn't something positive in it to be thankful for. Robinson Crusoe practiced in his adversity an attitude and action worthy of emulation, for no life is without its shipwrecks, its misfortunes.

For some people, limitations and adversities lie in their personal relationships: A life that wanted love and missed it; a home where marriage might have been a thing of beauty and was a bitter disappointment; a family where a child was greeted as a blessing and became an inward agony; a household where death has severed a tie that was the glory of the home.

Others are born with limited endowments, physically

and intellectually. Others suffer crippling illness or accident. Some spend years in environments that impede their highest development. Among the few things that are true of all of us is that each of us has to deal with handicap.

We don't know why it is, but some of life's most revealing insights and prods toward greater usefulness come to us not from life's loveliness, but from its deprivations, problems, and pain. Emerson informs us that, "Every evil to which we do not succumb is a benefactor."

William Wilberforce, for instance, was a diminutive man who never knew good health. For twenty years on doctor's orders he took opium to keep body and soul together, and had courage never to increase the dose. Yet in his infirmity, he did more than any other Englishman to stop the British slave trade. James Boswell went to hear him speak and said afterward, "I saw what seemed a mere shrimp mounted upon the table; but as I listened he grew, and grew until the shrimp became a whale."

As one stands in Westminister Abbey beside the grave of "the Attorney General of the unprotected and of the friendless" one sees that that suffering life translated itself into a persistent, unconquerable sympathy with downtrodden people that a lusty bulk of a man in perfect health probably never would have felt.

Mark Twain spent his youth in what he called a down-at-the-heel, out-at-the-elbows, slave-holding Mississippi River town. When other boys were in high school, he was at work in a printing office. His university was the pilot's room on the top of a steamboat. His early environment was apparently as far from literature as the East is from the West, yet today it is easy for us to see that the first thirty years of his life were the very best possible preparation for his career as a man of letters. It is highly probable that saturating him with the formalism, the artificiality, and conventionality of an academic environment would have atrophied the spontaneity that made Mark Twain such an important maker of books.

No one can find greater joy than that which comes in taking a barren, desolate, and unpromising plant of life and making something productive and beautiful—something that would never have been at all, except for our effort. We must be hopeful gardeners of the spirit who know that without darkness, nothing comes to birth and without light, nothing flowers. The flowers may not be the kind we would have chosen, but our world becomes more beautiful because they blossom in it.

Being Faithful to Our Possibilities

OWHERE IN THE Bible are we encouraged to be a successful person. When I first became aware of this fact it came as something of a surprise. From our earliest hours we learn that our society gives high priority to success, keeping up with the Joneses, or being Number One.

The Bible does not teach that we are to be in competition with others, but we are called to be faithful to our own highest possibilities. What we are born with is God's gift to us. What we do with it is our gift to God and the world.

Each individual has a unique contribution to offer in life unlike that of any other. Rabbi Zusya, a famed rabbi who lived in Lithuania in the nineteenth century said, "On the day of judgment, God will not ask me why I had not been Moses but why I had not been Zusya."

The call to be faithful to our own highest possibilities is an unending quest. There are three simple but profound questions that, when asked and answered, give some indication of our faithfulness.

The first question is this: "What do those who know us

best think of us?" This is a searching question and a revealing one. There are those who are able to fool others at a distance. They are like the beautiful trees of fall. From a distance they appear magnificent and lovely in their many splendored colors, but on closer inspection, the trees are often discovered to be gnarled and rotten and not nearly as attractive as they seemed from afar.

We all know people we once admired who lost their luster when we came to know them better. Perhaps we discovered sham, hypocrisy, and pretense that were not discernible by lesser acquaintance.

First impressions are sometimes erroneous. A friend of mine with a sense of humor said of another, "When I first met him I didn't like him very much, but when I got to know him I didn't like him at all!"

Conversely, there are those we come to admire more as we come to know them better. We discover their little acts of kindness, caring, and love that were not publicized or widely known. A minister, conducting a memorial service, said of the deceased, "He always tried to be better than his friends believed him to be." Such a goal is worthy of emulation.

There are many compliments that may come to an individual in the course of a lifetime, but there is no higher tribute than to be loved most by those who know us best.

The second question in determining our faithfulness to our best is this: "What do we do with our time, energies, and resources? How do we invest them?" In the book of Genesis we read of the man named Methuselah who lived more than nine centuries. But other than length of days there was nothing of significance to report about him. He simply lived a long time. That was it.

I have been reading the autobiography of one of America's most eminent church historians, Dr. Roland Bainton (1894-1984). Dr. Bainton lived not nine centuries but nine decades and what amazingly productive years they were! His contribution to life left behind thirty-two books, 128 essays and articles, eighty book reviews, six book-length translations, a slide presentation of Christian history, hundreds of sermons preached, and a continuing contact with more than seven hundred of his former Yale Divinity School students. We marvel at and rejoice in what one devoted and hard-working individual can do.

Most of us do not have the potential to make such a phenomenal contribution to life, but it is heartening to know that faithfulness in offering even the smallest of gifts can be of value—a letter, a call, a kind word, a listening ear, a gift to a needy cause—such little acts of love and faithfulness make ours a better world.

The third question: "Why do we do what we do? What is our motive or intent?" It is possible to do the right thing for the wrong reasons. Our reasons for doing what we do are most revealing. At one time I believed I could tell a great deal about a person by looking him in the eye. I no longer believe that. I now believe I can know more about an individual by looking over his shoulder to observe what he is trying to do and become. It is that which most accurately defines him.

No one of us will ever be as good or as talented as we had hoped to be, but when we earnestly and continuously try to be faithful to our highest possibilities, some good will come.

J. Studdert Kennedy, chaplain of the British Royal Air Force in World War I, believed that at the end of life our creator will ask only one question:

"Well, what did you make of it?"

It is a fair question. We are still in the process of providing the answer.

❧

Compassion

ERHAPS THE FEATURE of our heritage as humans that can separate us most distinctively from other animals is the capacity to enter, by sympathetic imagination, into the experiences of others and thus magnify our own.

I say "perhaps" because a study of some animals does seem to reveal that there are animals besides humans that have the capacity to sense and feel the feelings of others. Whether their ability is through sympathetic imagination has not been determined.

At any rate, it can be said that the highest art of a human's life is the ability to empathize with the joys and sorrows of others. Empathy, the vicarious experiencing (within ourselves) of the feelings, thoughts, or attitudes of another, is more enduring and valuable than romantic love.

But compassion goes beyond even empathy, for it accompanies painful vicarious thoughts with a deep desire to alleviate the pain and remove its cause.

Dr. Leo K. Bustad, former dean of the School of Veterinary Medicine at Washington State University, has written a thoughtful book entitled, *Compassion: Our Last*

Great Hope. The book makes delightful reading, but the title itself is worth pondering. Compassion is an important but often overlooked necessity in a world of violence and callousness.

Bustad writes, "Unfortunately, our educational system is programmed to vaccinate us against empathy, against compassion, against working for the common good. The survival values that our society encourages the most are individualistic. We are trained to be cerebral, thick-skinned, and obsessed with ourselves."

This cerebral training is in opposition to what Ashley Montagu, the renowned anthropologist, believed the purpose of education to be. He wrote, "The main purpose of education is to teach a student to be a warm and caring human being."

"It could be argued," Montagu continued, "that education is a failure no matter what it has done for the head if it has done little or nothing for the heart—and it is possible to graduate with a degree in hand and be the possessor of an encyclopedic mind and still have a cold and uncaring heart."

One of the severest condemnations of many today is that they don't care what happens as long as it doesn't happen to them. "I don't know what apathy is," said one, "and I couldn't care less."

But people who are more highly sensitive to the good and beauty around them are often more sensitive to the suffering and pain, just as the ear that is most alive to harmony is most hurt by discord.

History's great personalities have not been victims of apathy. They have been burden-bearers, lifting the lives of others by their empathy and compassion. "Jesus wept." Only two words, but they provide a profound insight into the compassion of Jesus. Of him it was said, "Surely, he has borne our grief and carried our sorrows."

Tolstoy called Lincoln "the miniature Christ" because he identified with sorrow and grief wherever it existed. "I have not suffered by the South," said Lincoln. " I suffered with the South."

Jane Addams came from a family of privilege and affluence, but she did not let that privilege and affluence dull her sensitivity to the needs of the struggling immigrants in the Chicago area. She felt the pain of others in her own heart and decided to do something about it, founding the world-famous Hull House, one of the first social settlement houses in the United States.

Addams established a great variety of programs at Hull House, from day nursery to college courses, among people of every nation, race, and social class. Her caring, compassionate work was of such great worth that she shared the Nobel Peace prize in 1931 with Nicholas Murray Butler.

We may not be able to take away another person's grief and pain, but we may share it. A German proverb says a sorrow shared is a sorrow halved, and a joy shared is a joy doubled.

There are no specialists in compassion. Every human being possesses some measure of ability to care. Compassion is not confined to any age. A five-year-old girl came home from visiting in the house where her little friend had died. "Why did you go?" questioned her father. "To comfort her mother," was the little girl's reply. "What could you do to comfort her?" She said, "I climbed into her lap and cried with her."

> *If I can stop one Heart from breaking*
> *I shall not live in vain*
> *If I can ease one Life the Aching*
> *Or cool one pain*
> *Or help one fainting Robin*
> *Unto his Nest again*
> *I shall not live in Vain*

—*Emily Dickinson*

APRIL

Miracle of Spring

HE JOY OF the coming of springtime does some-thing for the soul. Hope, new life, color, warmth, possibility, anticipation—all are contained in the signs of spring.

It is invigorating to witness the amazing transformation in the world about us: the blooming crocus and the burst-ing tulips; newborn animals greeting the world; the crescendo of bird songs filling the air; brown hillsides changing their complexion. The flowering shrub, blossom-ing bush, and greening grass all declare their maker's praise and beautify the world we share.

Unfortunately, all do not grasp the awe and wonder of the season. Henry Wadsworth Longfellow wrote with sor-row of those who take the yearly change for granted or miss its wonder:

> If spring came but once in a century, instead of once a
> year, or burst forth with the sound of an earthquake, and
> not in silence, what wonder and expectation there would
> be in all hearts to behold the miraculous change! But
> now the silent succession suggests nothing but neces-

sity. To most men only the cessation of the miracle would be miraculous, and the perpetual exercise of God's power seems less wonderful than its withdrawal would be.

What delights sensitive souls in the spring is the appearance of beauty, but it is more than that. It is a hope beyond any visible reality. There is something in the softness of the air, in the lengthening of the days, in the very songs and fragrances of the springtime, that caresses us and consoles us after the cold rains and dark days of winter and assures us that life is good and the best is yet to be.

There is a danger that, in our preoccupation with the schedules and demands of this life, we may spend our days shuffling along with eyes to the ground, thinking about the day's busy agenda, never seeing the clouds, the birds on the trees or the birds in the sky, or passing heedlessly and unseeing while every common bush is aflame with the glory of God.

When we do step back and consider all of this, we discover that in all these little miracles of life there is a reminder that life is beautiful, full of possibility. As we watch the green stems push skyward and colorful petals unfold, nature reminds us that self-discovery is renewable and the development of our potential never ends.

No matter what our age or condition, there are still untapped possibilities within us, new beauty waiting to be born.

During moments when challenges are too great and burdens are too overwhelming, we must turn to the Creator who made all in the first place. And as we do, we have the faith that as God knows the intimate, wonderful details of nature, so He knows our human nature as well, and really loves and cares for us all. Only God can work the miracle of rejuvenation within, and God will do it.

That is why the miracles of springtime are such an inspiration. They testify that the Lord is present in the soul as well as in the soil, ready to give new birth to the way of love and beauty within us, while He is making a new world around us and beneath our feet in these beautiful spring days.

❧

Opening Up

OST OF US think of "shut-ins" as those who are compelled by sickness or injury to stay in the house, in a nursing or convalescent home. They are shut in, away from the busy life of the world beyond their own walls. They need, and deserve, the continuing care and love of us all.

But others make shut-ins of themselves—deliberately closing their eyes to the larger world beyond their own little sphere—and they are to be pitied.

In almost any American city, people can be found whose interests are circumscribed by their allegiance to their clubs. For them, those who do not belong to the club simply do not exist. More tragic is that occasionally the same spirit prevails in religious groups.

Devotion to one's own church or synagogue is a noble characteristic. Yet limiting our contacts to its membership short-circuits the good that can be done by united effort. Affirmations of common concern can be made together without betraying the integrity of faiths held separately.

One of the hopeful features of our time is the growing amount of shared concern among people of many faiths and ideologies about the scourges of humankind—hunger, homelessness, environmental problems, drug abuse, discrimination, the proliferation of guns, injustice, and war. Two great enemies of humanity are blind patriotism and religious exclusiveness. Certainly, I can know God within my own communion, but only a bit of God. I can love my neighbors in my own land, but only a few of them. No one religion has all the truth. We have much to learn from one another.

Christian missionaries have gone out on fire to convert the lost in other lands and have returned home in growing numbers with their own faith strengthened and clarified by the impact upon them of other great religions. Christians, too receive a fresh view of Jesus by the abandonment of the old, harsh proselytizing of the Jews in favor of the recognition that Christianity and Judaism are two faiths with a common center.

Inviting people to open the door to a large world is part of the mission of all creative religion. Happy are the communions that have such leaders. John Henry Jowett was such a man. He was the great British preacher who ministered at the Fifth Avenue Presbyterian Church in New York City, then returned to his native land and to Westminster Chapel in London.

Week after week, he encouraged his parishioners to see beyond the walls of their own church and nation. Once he told his congregation of making a call on a parish member in his little furniture-repair shop by the sea. Sitting on a work bench he had watched the man at his work and listened to the steady beat of the hammer. Little by little, the monotony of the work, the narrowness of the shop and the dimness of the light began to depress the preacher.

At length he asked, "Man, doesn't it bother you to work in such a confining space?" Brushing the sawdust from his apron, the craftsman replied as he reached over and opened the door. "When I get feeling bothered like that, pastor, I do as you have suggested—I open the door."

Glancing out the doorway the two men found themselves looking out over the open fields to the endless sea beyond.

Jawett said the little room was glorified by the larger view, the vastness of the fields, the sky, and the rolling sea. The surroundings of the room, so confining and bothersome, were banished by opening the door to a full range of creation and life.

One of the most dramatic stories of refusal to accept a confining horizon is that of Moses. The gist is packed into one sentence about Moses in the Book of Acts in the New Testament: "When Moses was forty years old, it came into his heart to visit his brethren, the sons of Israel." Moses left the confines of the palace of privilege and went to the brickyard where his people were enslaved.

Here, life began at forty for Moses. He opened the door onto a larger world of need, and he decided to share the lot of his people, and eventually led them to freedom.

Years ago the world was fascinated by the discovery of the mummy of a young prince of Egypt, Tutankhamen, preserved in a gold decorated coffin. Dr. Holford Luccock, one-time professor at Yale Divinity School, reminded us that Moses, too would have been a mummy in a gold coffin if he had not extended his horizon.

But Moses did not want to be a mummy. He preferred

to be a part of life reaching beyond the bondage that enslaved his people. That is the choice we all must make: to be some kind of a mummy, insulated by wrappings of a narrow sarcophagus or to push back our boundaries and identify with the promises and problems of our world.

When I was a senior in high school one of the assignments of our English class was the memorization of the last twelve lines of Edna St. Vincent Millay's marvelous poem, "Renascene." I will always be indebted to my teacher for opening the door on those magnificent lines. They have offered wise counsel for more than half a century of living:

> *The world stands out on either side*
> *No wider than the heart is wide;*
> *Above the world is stretched the sky,—*
> *No higher than the soul is high.*
> *The heart can push the sea and land*
> *Farther away on either hand;*
> *The soul can split the sky in two,*
> *And let the face of God shine through.*
> *But East and West will pinch the heart*
> *That cannot keep them pushed apart;*
> *And he whose world is flat—the sky*
> *Will cave in on him by and by.*

❧

No Small Parts

HREE WEEKS AGO my wife and I attended a concert at Meany Hall on the campus of the University of Washington. The featured soloist was a tenor of twenty-seven years. He was outstanding, but it was his accompanist who captured my imagination and admiration.

He was an unassuming young man, but highly talented. He had mastered the skill of being the unobtrusive servant of another's art. He was sensitive to the singer's phrasing, accent, timing—always watching the face, listening to the breathing.

It was his supportive role that helped make the evening a delight. He accepted the fact that as an accompanist he would succeed to the degree that he was forgotten.

But he did not go unnoticed. The singer invited the accompanist on stage with him for curtain calls, and then, stepping aside, he pointed to him in gratitude. The generous applause that followed gave evidence that the audience was not unaware of the important role he played.

It is reassuring to know that a person does not have to be a star to be useful. Giving the support that enables another to succeed is one of the finest expressions of humility, love, and unselfishness.

Dr. Halford Luccock, a long-time professor at Yale Divinity School, tells of a college commencement in which a young man graduated with high honors. There was in the audience a great musician—his mother. For years she had rendered notable music on two remarkable musical instruments—a typewriter and a washboard—the melodious accompaniment which made his education possible.

An Ivy League professor who made a study of National Merit Scholarship winners discovered that behind every one of those high-school young people there was an individual—a mother, a father, teacher, coach, pastor, scoutmaster, Camp Fire leader—someone who really cared, who continually encouraged excellence, never letting a student be satisfied with mediocrity.

Robert Brookfield, an actor, was once mistakenly reported to be dead. He had the rare experience of seeing his own obituary. It read: "Never a great actor, he was invaluable in supporting roles." Though he might not have considered that a compliment, nothing finer could be said of anyone—*invaluable in supporting roles.*

"We can't all be heroes," remarked Will Rogers, "because somebody has to sit on the curb and clap as they go by."

Often those who serve in supportive roles go unheralded, but without them others would not succeed.

Joe Montana, of the San Francisco 49ers football team, is a great quarterback. All sports-minded Americans know his name, but there are relatively few who could list the names of one or more of the offensive linemen who protected Montana, making it possible for him to throw a record number of touchdown passes in Super Bowl XXIV. It is to the credit of Montana that he constantly speaks of his teammates when commendation is directed his way. "Football," he says, "is a team sport. No one can play it alone."

Great scientists have been quick to acknowledge their indebtedness to others. Jonas Salk said the work he was able to do depended on the research of hundreds of men and women whose names remain unknown, but whose labors made possible the polio vaccine. Sir Isaac Newton said, "If I have seen further it is by standing on the shoulders of Giants."

More and more it is becoming obvious that great social change is not traceable to the skills of leaders so much as to the concern of millions of unknown individuals who cry out for justice and freedom. Winston Churchill was aware of this truth. He said it was the British people who had the lion's heart. It was his good luck to provide the roar.

In religion, too, great contributions have been made by those most of us have never heard of. The name David Livingstone is known to millions of people, but only a few have ever heard of David Hogg. He was the Sunday-school teacher in Scotland who instilled in Livingstone the sense of self-worth and desire to serve that encouraged the missionary to serve the needs of thousands in Africa.

Most of us will never be famous or widely known, but it is heartening to know that no one is useless who encourages and enables others to realize their best. A subordinate role is not a consolation prize, but an opportunity to meet the needs of others in unheralded but important ways.

In Oliver Goldsmith's poem, "The Deserted Village," he describes the parson whose philosophy is worth emulating:

> *Unpracticed he to fawn, or seek for power,*
> *By doctrines fashioned to the varying hour;*
> *For other aims his heart had learned to prize,*
> *More skilled to raise the wretched than to rise.*

❦

"We Are Members One of Another"

SOME YEARS AGO a telephone operator in a small Cape Cod town received a daily call from a man who asked the exact time. This went on for many weeks. Finally the operator asked the caller why he called every day requesting the right time. "Because," responded the caller, "I am the man responsible for blowing the whistle at noon each day."

"Well, that's mighty odd," the operator replied, "because every day, exactly at noon, I set my clock by your whistle."

A simple story, but an accurate parable of life. We are dependent on one another, and each life has more far-reaching effect on others than is often ever realized. Emerson enlarged this truth in his poem, "Each and All":

> *Nor knowest thou what argument*
> *Thy life to thy neighbor's creed has lent.*
> *All are needed by each one;*
> *Nothing is fair or good alone.*

It is a mark of humility and maturity to know how dependent we are. Not all reach that level of modesty and maturation. One man boasted that he was a self-made man. "Too bad," remarked one who was not impressed. "He should have called in some help."

As we grow in recognition of our interdependence we deepen our gratitude for what others have contributed to our welfare. We are carried out of ourselves beyond self-centered egotism so that we acknowledge that other lives have blended with ours, enriching us in countless ways.

Marian Anderson, the great contralto who died in April a year ago, usually used the impersonal "we" instead of "I" in her conversation. It gave her speech a touch of formality that some found objectionable. During a trip to Asia she was questioned about this habit by a Buddhist scholar.

Anderson replied, "One realizes, the longer one lives, that there is no particular thing that one can do alone. Many people are involved in the work we do—those who wrote the music, those who made the pianos on which the accompanist plays, and the accompanist who lends support to the performance. To go without any of these things, to stand on your own—even the voice, the breath—the everything—it is not your doing. So the 'I' is very small, after all."

Even so, the small "I" is very important. The smallest hair casts a shadow. One life can make a difference, no matter how insignificant it may seem to be. But humble people often believe they are not fit to have an influence. They believe they have quite enough to do in taking care of themselves and do not choose to be an example for others.

Humility is a virtue—a virtue we choose. However, when we look into the reality of influence, we see that influence is not a question of choice or conscious design. Influence is an inevitable and an inherent relationship from which we cannot escape. All we have to do is live and the influence of our lives is present—and will follow us.

This is what St. Paul meant when he said, "We are members one of another," in the 12th chapter of Romans. He wrote of it again in the 12th chapter of 1 Corinthians, enlarging on the concept. Here he uses members of our physical bodies to illustrate the truth that members of any kind of body are inextricably bound together, so that the health or disease of any part necessarily affects the whole.

The life of an entire community is sometimes transformed for good in its ideals and aims by those who have never thought of posing as a good example or setting a fine example but have simply gone on living in an elevating way others want to follow. (But it can probably also be said that the morale of an entire community is also greatly debased and weakened by a relatively few thoughtless, selfish, and self-serving individuals.) We can do more good by being good than in any other way.

Phillips Brooks, remembered as one of America's greatest church leaders of the nineteenth century, said, "No man or woman of the humblest sort can really be strong, gentle, pure, and good without the world being a better place for it, without someone being helped and comforted by the very existence of that goodness."

Brooks, himself, was such a person. A perplexed student once went with his questions to the office of the great clergyman. After the interview, the young man realized that he had not asked his questions. "But it doesn't matter," he thought. "What I needed was not the solution to a special problem but the contagion of a triumphant spirit."

Every soul that touches yours—
Be it the slightest contact—
Get there from some good;
Some little grace; one kindly thought;
One aspiration yet unfelt;
One bit of courage
For the darkening sky;
One gleam of faith
To brave the thickening ills of life;
One glimpse of brighter skies
To make this life worth while
And heaven a surer heritage.

—George Eliot
"Making Life Worthwhile"

The Art of Living

SOME WEEKS AGO while reading a magazine, I saw a heading on one of the articles that arrested me as firmly as if a policeman had laid his hand on my shoulder. The heading was, "I'm Not Sorry that He Died."

Ordinarily, we are sorry when someone dies, so I read the story to discover what the headline meant.

It told of a twenty-three-year-old man who had been reared in a home where he was neither wanted nor loved. As a consequence, he was left to his own devices.

Seeking recognition wherever he could find it, he fell into evil habits and ran afoul of the law. He served time in a reform school, then couldn't find a job when he got out. Soon he was back in prison. Released again, he bought a gun, and was killed trying to rob someone.

"I'm not sorry that he died," the writer said, adding, "I'm sorry that he never lived."

Unfortunately, the same arresting sentence could be written about many others who have been born into more favorable circumstances. Life is a gift to us all, but some face it as though it were a sentence. They have more to live with, but less to live for, and are either fed up at fifteen or burned out at forty.

Heywood Broun refused to return to the twentieth reunion of his college class because, he said, he didn't want to mingle with dead men. That was a strong judgment, perhaps unjustified in all cases, and yet we know it comes close enough to the truth to be disconcerting.

Thoreau went visiting in New York City and summed up his impressions in one sentence: "I walked through New York City yesterday and met no real and living person."

A man as sincere and close to nature as Thoreau probably sensed the pretense, fear, and insecurity in the faces of the people he passed.

Again, the joyful words of Psalm 118 can save us from joining the ranks of those unburied dead. "This is the day that the Lord has made; let us rejoice and be glad in it."

What a beautiful way to greet the dawn! I admit that I am not one who by nature bounds out of bed. My alarm clock wakes me up, but it doesn't turn me on.

Sometimes I am grateful that God arranged it so we get out of bed only once a day. As I have said before, Psalm 118 has been an enormously effective motivator for me. But still, there are mornings that look like they have been up all night—dark, rainy, and cold—and it almost seems a sacrilege to attribute them to the Lord. "This," I say, "is the day the Lord hath made?"

When tempted in that direction, I think of the little girl whose mother asked her to offer grace at breakfast. "We thank you, dear God," she began, "for this beautiful day."

"Bless you, my dear," said her mother, "for offering the prayer, but apparently you didn't look outdoors before you prayed. It is a dismal day."

"Mother," responded the little girl, "never judge a day by its weather."

The art of living is to discover how to see, not merely look; to hear, not merely listen.

One man who knew that so well was William Lyon Phelps. Phelps was a literature professor at Yale University in the early 1900s, but what he really taught was compassion.

"I never go to a store, a hotel, or a barbershop," he said, "without saying something agreeable to everyone I meet. I'll ask a barber if he doesn't get tired standing on his feet all day. I ask him how he came to take up barbering, how long he's been at it. How many heads of hair he has cut. When I meet a man on the street with a beautiful dog I always comment on the dog's beauty. As I walk on, I frequently glance back over my shoulder and many times have seen the man admiring and petting his dog. My appreciation has renewed his appreciation."

❧

May

The Simple Life

BEGAN THIS YEAR with a firm resolution to simplify my life. We are now entering the fifth month and I confess that I have not achieved my goal in the manner I had hoped.

Discovering a way to live simply is one of life's most complicated problems. For me, there has always been more to do than I have been able to get done. I have tried to take one day at a time, but sometimes it seems as though several days attack me at once. Before I have been able to do what I wanted to do, there has always been something I have had to do first.

I suspect that the problems I have encountered trying to live the simple life are common problems. The reasons for our inability to achieve the goal of simplicity are many. Most of us would admit that our lives are cluttered with more things than we actually need. I empathize with those whose work is in merchandising. It is a demanding vocation, and my hat is off to those who undertake it. Yet, I believe that Americans have no idea how we have been debauched by the incessant clatter of buy, buy, buy.

Possessing so many things, it is easy to lose sight of

intellectual and spiritual values, and to become shallow and superficial materialists. We work ourselves into high blood pressure by piling up mountains of largely meaningless odds and ends, like so many pack rats, giving all too little thought to what we, ourselves, would really like to get out of life.

The Archbishop of Canterbury said, "I don't even read advertisements. I could spend all my life wanting things." John Stuart Mill, the brilliant English philosopher and economist, had an even better idea. He said, "I've learned to seek my happiness in limiting my desires rather than by attempting to satisfy them."

The quest of the simple life is further compounded in that we have built an altar to energy and made activity our lord. We have more labor-saving devices and less time than any other generation. We have increased our resources and lessened our resourcefulness. Our crowded schedules and hectic pace bring anxiety and apprehension to millions of people. A man in Washington, D.C., said, "I'm nervous so much of the time, that when I'm not nervous, then I get nervous."

Dr. Norman Vincent Peale has pointed out that people today live such crowded lives that we no longer see them sleeping—even in church.

Several years ago, the street railway authorities of an American city tried to relieve the crowded subway by inaugurating an advertising campaign calling attention to the light, the air, and the scenery of its surface lines. But the effort was a failure, because, in the minds of most Americans, no advantage can compensate for the lack of speed.

A young woman is reported to have made it through the Metropolitan Art Gallery in New York in thirty minutes. She said she would have made it in twenty, except that she had on her high heels! It is not unusual to see someone running up an escalator. We wonder what is done with all the time that is saved.

Those who learn to live lives of simplicity and calm learn how to choose between what is primary and what is secondary; between what is urgent and what can wait; between what is of great value and what is of little consequence. They learn the art of a selective procrastination—putting off indefinitely what they never really need to do at all.

They are not lazy. They know it is important to be busy, but not too busy. When too many irons are in the fire, the fire will go out. These folks are not hermits. They know the human spirit needs associations that enrich life and give it meaning. They are friendly to all, but they nurture a few close friendships. They do not run all of the way to the grave, knowing that if they do not pause, nothing worthwhile will catch up with them.

They know the value of a wise passiveness and a quiet receptivity, and recognize the need for isolation, for an insulation against nonessentials, and an openness to the eternal. With a reasoned pace, they have time for the little acts of love and kindness that are the best parts of a good person's life.

We would all serve ourselves and others more effectively if we followed a common rule for our daily lives. Try to do less and do it better. God does not judge us by the multitude of works we perform, but how well we do the little duties that are ours. There is no point served in covering a lot of ground if we cultivate but little of it and fail to see or smell the flowers along the way. The object should be not so much to get through a great deal of work, but to do the few things we have to do well.

∗

Pick of the Litter

E ARE A nation of animal lovers. Turnstiles tell us that animal watching at our zoos attracts more people than any other spectator sport.

Each of us has a favorite animal. Harry Truman, who lived on Mount St. Helen's before it erupted, owned fifteen cats.

My favorite pet has always been a dog. Looking back across the years, I see how very important dogs have been in my life. I had been an ordained minister only a few weeks when I received a phone call from Larry Chisholm, an eight-year-old boy. His dog had just been killed by a car. "Mr. Turner," he sobbed, "do you conduct funerals for dogs? I do not want to bury my dog without some kind of ceremony."

Seminary had not prepared me for such an eventuality, and I was nonplussed. Remembering the Scripture's affirmation of God's care when even a sparrow falls to the ground, I replied, "Why not?" I conducted a service, reading Scripture, reciting a poem and offering a prayer. As we walked from the burial plot, my young friend asked, "Mr. Turner, are there any dogs in heaven?"

I was not ready for that, either, and I am afraid my answer was less than satisfactory. At least, my innate love for dogs enabled me to console him to some degree.

Through the years, our family has had a succession of dogs, and each one was special. It was our most recent pet that I remember most vividly. Our dachshund Gretta had died, and we were eager to bring another dog to our home. We went to the pound to claim another dachshund pictured in the paper.

But by the time we arrived the dog had been claimed. A Manchester terrier puppy, sensing our mission, thrust her nose through the wire fence. The plaintive look in her eyes seemed to say, "Pick me." Our children did—and promptly named her "Pick."

I had read that forty percent of Americans owned dogs and vice versa, and I began to understand what that meant. Pick thought she was one of us.

Each evening, Pick waited for my arrival home. She'd wag her tail as if to say, "Welcome." "Pick," I'd say, "you've got it made. Other animals work for their keep. A canary sings, cows give milk, and chickens lay eggs, but you don't have to do anything."

Undaunted, she seemed to reply, "That's not true, I give love, and that's something. Besides, when you roll on the floor with me and make a fool of yourself, I make a fool of myself, too, and pretend to enjoy it. Furthermore, I don't tell anyone beyond the walls of this home what we do." She had a point.

After fourteen years, Pick had a series of convulsions. Our veterinarian counseled that it would be merciful to have her "put to sleep." It was an agonizing decision, but one that had to be made. When the hour arrived, Pick and I drove off in our car as we had done countless times before, but this was to be our last ride together. I left her and drove directly to my study, and there, alone, I cried for fully an hour.

A parishioner sent me a consoling poem titled: "Message From a Little Ghost."

> *I've explained to St. Peter I'd rather stay here*
> *Outside the Pearly Gate.*
> *I won't be a nuisance, I won't even bark.*
> *I'll be very patient—and wait.*
> *I'll be here and chew a celestial bone,*
> *No matter how long you may be.*
> *I'd miss you so much—if I went in alone,*
> *It wouldn't be heaven for me.*

I was mourning for nearly a week, but then, amazingly, I had a dream. I saw Pick with many other dogs at heaven's gate. They were rollicking together in friendly play, each awaiting the arrival of its master.

When I awoke from that dream, my mourning had ended. I wished I could see Larry again to give him a better answer than I had given forty years before.

❦

Ordinary People

UR TECHNOLOGICAL AGE, with its emphasis on computers, speed, and masses of numbers and data, has the tendency to make individuals feel insignificant. Many feel they are little cogs in a huge impersonal wheel or simply an extension of an inanimate machine.

A sign in a Defense Department office in Washington D.C., warns: "Look alive. You can be replaced by a button." It isn't that simple. Every individual is of worth. Everyone is someone.

Society is still made up of individuals, and everything good in society comes from the multiplying power of single units. We, of course, need great leaders, but we are not saved by leaders alone. A nation is made strong by the courage and integrity of millions of ordinary people.

Excellence is a commendable goal, and there is a sense in which, for the good of society, A's ought to be more valued than C's and home runs more noteworthy than singles. But no one should be discouraged if he is not unusually bright or endowed with superior attributes.

Oliver Wendell Holmes said something to the effect

that one of the great reliefs of life is to discover your own mediocrity. But mediocrity does not mean insignificance. A dull axe can hew a walkable trail. A person is foolish not to be what he can be simply because he can't be what he would be.

Significant contributions to the world do not wait to be done by perfect people. "How silent the woods would be if only the best birds sang."

Our superstar culture is unfair and destructive to the spirit of many youngsters in the arbitrary way it reserves affirmation only for the exceptionally beautiful, the unusually brilliant, or outstandingly competent. Ordinary people have worth, too, and must not be intimidated or immobilized by the scholars and top achievers. Skill and brilliance do not mean an individual contributes beneficially to the world, nor does average endowment mean a mediocre performance.

Any student of history knows that the largest part of the useful work of the world has been done by people of average talent, but extraordinary dedication. A study of one thousand eminent men and women listed in the *Dictionary of American Biography* reveals that only forty-eight were especially promising in their youth.

To our country's credit, we have decided that determining the guilt or innocence of humans is a thing too important to be trusted to trained men and women. For that task, we enlist people who know no more law than you or I, but who can feel what must be felt in the jury box.

When it wants a library catalogued or a solar system discovered, or any trifle of that kind, it uses up its specialists. But when it wishes something done that is really serious, it collects twelve of the ordinary men and women and summons them to duty. The founder of Christianity did the same. His disciples were men of ordinary endowments, but extraordinary commitment and power.

In the long run, matters of faith and morals will not be defended or witnessed by the philosophers and theologians alone, important as they are in formulating and verbalizing what we believe. The salient truths of the great faiths will be kept alive by the common people. In every generation there are a few exceptional souls, the four-leaf clovers, as it were, in the field of life. But the clovers that keep the fields green, feed the cows and bees, giving us milk and honey, are the plain folks.

One may desire to accomplish great and noble tasks, but the big souls are those who tackle humble tasks as though they were great and noble. The world is moved along toward worthy goals not only by the mighty shoves of its heroes, but also by the aggregate and tiny pushes of each honest worker. "I must do something" will always solve more problems than, "Something must be done."

"I am only one," wrote Edward Everett Hale, "but I am one. I can't do everything, but I can do something. What I can do I ought to do, and what I ought to do by the grace of God I will do."

Who to Trust?

WAS REARED IN a home where love was central but trust was the key word in our family training. We never locked our doors or windows. My mother and father believed and taught that the only way to make a person trustworthy was to trust that person. My brothers and sister and I were given many liberties and we were trusted to use our freedom intelligently and believe that others would do the same. I often heard my father say, "The person who trusts nobody is apt to be the person nobody trusts."

The lesson of trust was so deeply ingrained in my being that I have had great difficulty making the transition into our age of locked doors, burglar alarms, and distrust of strangers.

My early training worked against me one evening when I went to Virginia Mason Hospital to attend a class of instruction for diabetics.

I parked my car on Seneca Street near Boren, leaving my briefcase in the unlocked car. When I returned to the car at 9:00 P.M., the briefcase and its contents were gone. A search in the bushes nearby was to no avail.

Although nothing was taken that I cannot live without, it was a discombobulating experience, for in the briefcase had been three stamped, unmailed letters and two finished manuscripts for talks I was scheduled to give within the next two weeks.

Fortunately, I had carried with me my billfold with some money and credit cards and my car keys. But several other important items were in the briefcase—most important, my date book that contained not only my appointments for weddings, luncheon engagements, counseling, and speaking commitments, but addresses and telephone numbers.

Woe is me! I live in fear each day as I sit uneasily in my office vaguely remembering I have a luncheon meeting or counseling session with someone, but not remembering the specifics—the who, what, where, and when. Luckily, my wife and I coordinate our calendars enough so that we more or less know how to get in touch with one another, but names and telephone numbers of my appointments are seldom in her datebook.

I am grateful for my early training in trust. I have no animosity for the one who took my briefcase. The person apparently needed something, or thought he or she did. I only feel sorry for whoever it was and hope the need was a legitimate one and will one day be met without the necessity of having to steal from another.

I do not want to make invalid my parents' admonition to trust, by becoming cynical and mistrusting and believing that society as a whole is not trustworthy. Such a conclusion would be a fallacy of sampling, a distortion of truth. On the very night my briefcase was stolen, presumably by one person, there were more than a million people in the Puget Sound area who did not steal a briefcase or violate a trust of any kind.

My confidence in people's integrity was confirmed by a news release from upper Michigan that told of an unattended fruit and vegetable roadside stand that had a sign on the table that read: "Please take what you need and leave what you feel it is worth in the container at the end of the table. Thank you."

The proprietor reported that more money was left in the till than would have been received in a person-to-person transaction, and he had no reason to believe any money was ever taken.

Whereas I believe most people are honest, I recognize that there are people who think of themselves as honest, but perhaps aren't quite.

The IRS once received an envelope with an unsigned note and a $100 bill enclosed. The note read: "Last year I falsified my tax report and I have been unable to sleep. Please find enclosed $100. If I still can't sleep, I will send the rest of the money."

And a friend told me of a ticket seller at a ball game who received a $20 bill for a ticket that cost $14. The buyer walked away, forgetting his change, and the seller tried to get his attention by knocking on the window—with a sponge.

These bits of humor are simply the exceptions that prove the rule. Most people are honest, but how do we account for the lack of trust that permeates our society today?

Are the unmet needs of humans so great and the

opportunities for fulfillment of those needs so few that cheating and stealing are encouraged? Is training for honesty neglected in home, religious institutions, and schools?

Whatever our reasons for lack of trust, it is sad, because trust is the central ingredient in all civilized societies. Trust is at the heart of all family and friendship relationships.

The glory of friendship is not the outstretched hand, nor the kindly smile, nor the joy of companionship; it is the spiritual inspiration that comes to one when you discover that someone not only loves you, but trusts you as well. It is the greatest compliment we can receive or give to another.

> *Better trust all and be deceived,*
> *And weep for trust and the deceiving,*
> *Than doubt one heart that when believed*
> *Would bless one's life with that believing.*
>
> *Oh, in this mocking world too fast*
> *The doubting fiend o'ertakes our youth;*
> *Better to be cheated to the last*
> *Than lose the blessed hope of truth.*

—*Frances Anne Kemble*

A Day for Remembering

E HUMANS ARE unique among all living creatures in our instinct to preserve the memory of ourselves. We are the only animals that bury our dead, build tombs, and mark our graves.

We write books, give gifts, and endow institutions not only to help worthy causes, but to assure our perpetuity.

It is sweet to be remembered, bitter to be forgotten. Men in prison have begged for names, not numbers. When we address another by name we affirm his dignity and identity. When we remember another after he is gone we testify to his worth.

Several years ago, I returned to college after an absence of many years. A professor greeted me by name. "Dr. Glauner," I said, "I'm surprised and gratified that, after all these years, you still remember my name."

"Dale," he said with a twinkle, "I always remember the real good students and the real bad ones." I didn't have the courage to pursue that further. Suffice it to say, I was glad to be remembered.

Congress showed some wisdom in designating a national day of remembering. It began as a day for memorializing our war dead, but has been expanded to include all loved ones who have gone before us. That Memorial Day has degenerated into little more than an excuse for a three-day holiday does not remove the need to remember.

We live in an era of exaggerated speech. Extravagant claims bombard our senses daily. "You are what you eat," they say. "You are what you wear [or drive, or feel]." All of these overstate to make a point. But it is an altogether different claim to say that we are what we remember. If we could know what another person has remembered and forgotten, we would know that person quite well.

Some people, for example, nurture memories of a wrong committed against them. They build a thirst for revenge and live to slake that thirst. Francis Bacon wrote, "He that studieth revenge keepeth his wounds green, which otherwise would heal and do well."

In other ways, memory plays a much more positive role. It was vital, for instance, in keeping biblical history alive. The Hebrew word "zachar," the verb "to remember," is an exceedingly dominant verb in the Old Testament. It was critical for Israel not to forget its past. Scriptures were recited and liturgical acts stimulated the memory of God's leadership.

Remembering our secular, national heritage is important, too. Do you remember John Adams' "Apostrophe to Posterity"? "Posterity," he thundered, "you will never know how much it cost the present generation to preserve your freedom! I hope you will make good use of it. If you do not, I shall repent it in heaven that I ever took half the pains to preserve it." That was nearly two centuries ago. Think of the cost since that day.

I confess that I am ill at ease with the "hawkish" stands of the American Legion and the Veterans of Foreign Wars, but I am grateful to these organizations for reminding us of our indebtedness to the thousands of men and women who died at war to win and preserve our freedom. No one of us can fully repay that debt.

"All of history," wrote Richard Neuhaus, "is one endless massacre stretching back to the dawn of mankind. Wherever we are in history we stand on a mountain of corpses—and however terrible the thought, we are the beneficiaries of all this carnage."

It is a terrible thought, and because it is we long for the day when wars will cease and the symbols for peace will be as strong and as emotionally moving as those that catapult us into war. Doves and olive branches are no match for marching bands, uniforms, flags, and banners.

We remember our war dead most constructively when we work and pray for the peace for which they died. When this becomes our goal, Memorial Day becomes not merely a holiday, but a holy day, and we are closer to the lasting peace for which we yearn.

❧

JUNE

Education After Graduation

MANY YEARS AGO, one of my friends, Guy Keeler, delivered a high school commencement address on "The Marks of an Educated Man." The next day the local newspaper detailed his speech under the heading: "Guy Keeler's Commencement Address Reveals Need for Education."

Regardless of the paper's unintentional comment on Keeler's educational status, his theme, at least, is worth pondering as school draws to a close.

The purpose of education is not just to impart knowledge. We are not intended to be walking encyclopedias. Schooling is designed to whet the appetite for more learning, develop the ability to distinguish good from evil, and encourage us to incarnate moral values and caring spirits.

The educated man is the one who controls circumstances instead of being mastered by them. He knows that life is not intended to be endured, but redeemed. He meets all occasions bravely and acts intelligently. He is always honorable and he faces disagreeable situations good-naturedly. He holds pleasures under control and is neither overcome by misfortune nor spoiled by success.

No amount of classroom time or degrees received assures that a person has realized these qualities of charac-ter or gifts of mind. Dr. Robert Hutchins, a former president of Chicago University, said, "Some graduates are given a sheepskin to cover their intellectual nakedness. It is possible to have a diploma under the arm and very little under the skull." Likewise, a person who lacks formal training is not necessarily mediocre or inept. Many of the world's most productive personalities have had only limited schooling. Winston Churchill, for instance, as well as Will Rogers, Irving Berlin, Walt Disney, Frank Lloyd Wright, Pablo Picasso, and Henry Ford, never went beyond high school.

It was experience, industriousness, perseverance, curiosity, ingenuity, and self-disciplined study that enabled each of them to make significant contributions to life.

Muhammad Ali, speaking at Harvard Business School in 1975, said, "I didn't go to college and Jesus never went to school and Moses was so dumb he couldn't even talk, but they're great because God manifests himself through what you might consider to be nothing."

True, God can speak through the lowliest and the least. But when skills are developed, the opportunities to serve are enhanced. "What we are born with is God's gift to us. What we do with it is our gift to God."

If there is anything education does not lack today, it is critics. No one would claim that schools are perfect, but basically they are organized to do everything possible to encourage our development. Unfortunately, like Chicken Little, some detractors have reacted before they had all the facts. For them, it has been easier to be critical than it has been to be correct.

Fortunately, thousands of dedicated, competent teachers and administrators are laboring effectively without complaint, though many are underpaid.

A student's life is no easier—and often no more appreciated. The student's role needs to be seen as an occupation. Those who take the occupation seriously work as hard and with as much tension, and greater consequence of failure, as do people in the conventional labor force.

The time those student laborers spend in school in no way can be considered an interlude between childhood and the real world. The tensions of study and exams are heightened for most students in their realization that a job is not assured when schooling has ended.

Agnes W. Thomas wrote:

> *My daughter has her master's,*
> *My son his Ph.D.;*
> *But father is the only one*
> *Who has a J-O-B.*

In any case, it's good for all of us to remember that education is an ongoing process in which God's universe is the classroom. The greater the island of knowledge, the longer the shoreline of wonder. Will Durant said: "Sixty years ago I knew everything. Now I know nothing. Education is a progressive discovery of our own ignorance."

This is not an invitation to despair. It is a call to adventure. The insatiable yearning to know more makes each day exciting and each new discovery a gem.

Staying Alive

URS IS A youth-obsessed society—a society in which the rewards and pleasures that come with growing old are often dismissed.

It seems that no one wants to grow old, and if there were to be a choice, it would certainly be to stay young forever. Mark Twain said we would be infinitely happier if we could be born at eighty and gradually approach eighteen.

As we grow older, we become increasingly aware that advancing years bring infirmities. Aging is defined as the time when almost everything hurts and what doesn't hurt won't work. When comedian Red Skelton was eighty years old, he was asked by an admirer to shake hands. Skelton replied, "At my age, you just hold it. It shakes itself."

Even though everyone wants to live a long time, nobody wants to be old. In fact, La Rochefoucauld, the great French writer of the seventeenth century, said, "Few people know how to be old."

However, as B. F. Skinner points out in his book, *Enjoy Old Age*, the young have their problems, too. A great many people will tell you they were miserable when they were young, and a surprising number between the ages of fifteen and twenty-four commit suicide.

"Thank God," said Rudyard Kipling, "we never have to suffer again as we did when we were young." And yet, it is probably easier to be happy when we are young. Few would agree with Rabbi Ben Ezra's description of the last of life as the part for which the first was made.

For young people to expect that "the best is yet to be" could be a great mistake. What comes with the passing of time can be enjoyed if we simply take a little extra thought and plan wisely. We can prepare for advancing years in the manner in which we live our daily lives.

We can take a lead from H. L. Mencken, who said, "We cannot do much about the length of our life, but we can do something about its width and depth." Reuel L. Howe, pastoral counselor and educator, bears this out, as follows:

> We all are accumulating birthdays. But we do not have to grow old in mind and spirit. Since the process of aging begins early, so should the preparation and planning of one's life for creative aging. Preparation for aging is like making an investment.
>
> When I buy stocks, bonds, real estate, or whatever, I hope for good dividends and profitable gains. So it is in aging. As early as possible in our life span we can make decisions and choose a way of life that will yield good returns and each year will add dividends of growing interest and personal satisfaction.

Studies at New York University and elsewhere show that people who are the least active mentally and physically age earlier, and are the most prone to disease. Research has shown also that just as lack of bodily activity has an adverse physical effect on us, failure to keep our minds actively engaged in mental work causes our mental powers to decline prematurely. It has been repeatedly shown that mental ability actually increases as a person grows older if the mind is kept busy. The opposite is true for the mentally lazy person.

When Franklin D. Roosevelt came to Washington, D.C., in 1933 to be inaugurated, he set aside time to call on Justice Oliver Wendell Holmes, then in the ninety-second year of his formidable life. Roosevelt found Justice Holmes in his library. "Why are you reading Plato, Mr. Justice?" Roosevelt asked.

Holmes replied, matter-of-factly, "I am trying to improve my mind. One's education must go on as long as we do."

When Socrates was an old man he found time to learn music and dancing and thought that his time was well-spent.

Roland Bainton, well-known church historian and professor at Yale Divinity School, wrote more books between his retirement at age sixty-eight and death at eighty-nine than he had in forty years of teaching.

Peter Ustinov's counsel is an infallible guidepost that merits emulation: "Since we live out our lives in the prison of our minds, our duty is to furnish them well."

The Syrian medieval mystic, Sir Isaac, wrote: "The ladder that leads to the Kingdom of Heaven is hidden within you, and is found in your own soul. Dive into yourself and you will discover the rungs to ascend."

An unknown author has written a prayer for those of us who are growing older:

God keep my heart attuned to laughter
    When youth is done;
When all the days are gray days, coming after
    The warmth, the sun.
God keep me from bitterness, from grieving,
    When life seems cold;
God keep me always loving and believing
    As I grow old.

What's Your Handicap?

N A WORLD of great diversity, there is one thing we all have in common. Each of us has a handicap of one kind or another. For some, it is a physical, mental or emotional infirmity; others suffer estrangements within the family circle; and there are others who struggle through a lifetime with feelings of inferiority or timidity. There are millions who suffer the handicaps that accompany economic privation.

As Thomas Gray walked through the softened twilight in the little churchyard at Stoke Poges, he remembered the village Hampdens, the mute inglorious Miltons and the obscure Cromwells of whose handicapped lives he said: "Chill penury repress'd their noble rage, And froze the genial current of the soul."

One has this handicap, and one that. The race of life is run in fetters. We are inspired and heartened by those who deal with this human predicament in creative and courageous ways, turning a minus into a plus and disadvantage into advantage.

The story of history is the story of those who refused to use handicap as an excuse for not contributing something worthwhile to life. They did not merely tie a knot in the end of the rope and hang on, but became masters rather than victims of circumstance. A library of books and papers could be assembled that tell of men and women who did not simply endure but prevailed in the presence of what could have been a crippling disability. John Milton, Ludwig van Beethoven, George Handel, Sir Walter Scott, Helen Keller, and Robert Louis Stevenson are but a few of those who are better known. Around us today there are family members and friends who bear their own burdens, handicaps, and infirmities without dramatizing them to others. They are the courageous souls who lift our lives by theirs.

Dean Briggs at Harvard had such people in mind when he responded to a freshman student who came to his office to explain his tardiness in submitting an assignment.

"I'm sorry," said the student, "but I was not feeling very well."

"Young man," replied Dean Briggs, "please bear in mind that the greater part of the world's work is carried on by people who aren't feeling very well."

What is the secret of positive response in the presence of handicap? We need first of all to know what our handicaps are. We must be honest with ourselves and know what it is that is within reason for us to accomplish and know what it is that is likely to be beyond us. It is wise not to move in areas where our abilities do not have some relationship to the demands of the task. God has endowed us with certain native abilities which are likely to respond to cultivation more readily than some others. Sometimes we can either develop a skill commensurate with the demands or we can eliminate some of the impediments that handicap us. Many handicaps can be minimized or removed by competent medical care, wise counsel, and concerted effort by the one in need. We recall the story of the farmer in Maine who was seated on a wagon drawn by two horses.

"Tell me," he called out to a bystander, "how long does this hill last?"

"Hill nothing," was the reply. "Your hind wheels are off!"

Even the casual observer was able to help that man know of his handicap. Sometimes a friend or enemy's comment can make us aware of ours. It is wisdom to know our limitations, change what can be changed, and learn to live positively with that which cannot be altered. God does not require perfection—only the best that we are able to do.

We must learn to see each handicap in larger perspective and not magnify it out of proportion to what ought to be its inhibiting power. A little child breaks a toy and his whole world is shattered. He is unable to see this one incident in perspective to the whole of life. Sometimes adults become frustrated, anxious, and defeated by handicaps that do not deserve centrality.

Charles Eliot, one of Harvard's great presidents, was born with a facial disfigurement. It could have been for him a handicap or a source of embarrassment, but he was fortunate to have a wise mother who said to him, "Son, it is not possible for you to get rid of this facial disfigurement. Surgeons say that nothing can be done, but it is possible for you, with God's help, to grow a mind and soul so big that people will forget to look at your face." He did just that and became an outstanding man and noted leader of American higher education.

See that eight-year-old boy seated at his desk in school? Could anyone be more unattractive or unpromising than this lad? He is pale, emaciated, has poor eyes, buck-teeth, and a frail body. But who could measure the boy's heart? Who could guess what Teddy Roosevelt would become?

As he matured, he came to believe that we act our way into right thinking more readily than we think our way into right acting. He demonstrated his conclusion in the manner in which he lived his life.

Roosevelt captured health by acting as though he were healthy. He overcame fear by acting as though he was not afraid. He overcame the lack of physical beauty by acting as though he was as attractive an anyone else. He did not dupe himself. He recognized his defeats and limitations, but he did not dwell on them or let them become a reason for justifying laziness, cowardice, or feelings of inferiority.

Creative and courageous personalities reveal that handicaps, far from being the curse they may seem to be, can be prods to the realization of our highest possibilities and greatest usefulness.

❧

Conquering Fate

DOCTORS HAVE SAID that the worst bruises our bodies can sustain are internal bruises. They reveal no signs to the casual observer. There is no discoloration of the flesh. There are few, if any, visible symptoms. Yet these same doctors assure us that the body has suffered injury.

It is a suggestive thought. Are not the heaviest hurts the human heart carries brought on by internal bruises, secret sorrows, personal pains, frustrated hopes, and unfulfilled longings and loneliness? The world seldom knows of them, or has forgotten about them. The symptoms are not visible to those hurrying past. But most of us, though we smile bravely, carry in our hearts and lives scars of secret sorrows and pain.

The poet Louise Driscoll expressed it poignantly:

> *God pity all the brave who go*
> *The common way, and wear*
> *No ribboned medals on their breasts,*
> *No laurels in their hair.*
>
> *God pity all the lonely folk*

With griefs they do not tell
Women waking in the night
And men dissembling well.

In common courage of the street
The crushed grape is the wine.
Wheat in the mill is daily bread
And given for a sign.

And who but God shall pity those
Who go so quietly
And smile upon us when we meet
And greet so pleasantly.

We may not know the specific hurts of those about us, but we can be certain the hurting is there.

Admirable as it is to not inflict our ills on others, the cause and nature of the pain that plagues us must be addressed by ourselves. Healing must be sought and an important question asked: How can we make a constructive response to the ills that afflict us?

For one thing, they must be faced with an attitude that is positive rather than negative. Isn't it true that life really does depend upon how we look at it? It is like a checkerboard, made up of black squares and red squares. Focus your attention on the dark squares, the hurts and sorrows long enough and life becomes a pretty mournful and depressing experience.

But there are brighter spots. No situation in our experience is so bad that it cannot be improved by the attitude with which we face it. Read again and sense the strength and sustaining power in Sarah Bolton's great poem, "The

Inevitable," with its memorable words: "He alone is great who by a life heroic conquers fate."

You know them and I know them: individuals who have faced the same kind of sorrow and endured the same hurts, and we have marveled, for one was felled and the other stood. And when we have thought about it, there was no rhyme or reason in the mystery of it all, except that one looked at it positively and one negatively.

Not only must our attitude toward these hurts of the body and heart be positive rather than negative, we must also make deliberate efforts to take our attention off ourselves and the frustration, pain, grief, and disappointment.

Jesus' words are psychologically sound: "He who would save his life must lose it." That is, we redeem ourselves from wretchedness by serving others. In getting ourselves off our hands, we make our lives richer and happier.

We don't have to go far to do this. Wherever we live or wherever we work there are those around us whose needs are as great as or greater than our own. There is healing power in the presence of those who express affection, caring, and commendation. This we can do. There are countless worthy causes needing support. In helping to heal the wounds of others, we are helping to heal our own ills.

Sit at home, if we will, and brood over our own lives, bemoan our own circumstance, nurse our own griefs and grudges, and don't think of anything but ourselves. Then there can be no measure of relief for the bitter sorrow or painful hurt.

But push out of this narrow room of mirrors in which we have found ourselves caught and in which we have seen only ourselves, and there will come to us a right and clear view and we will begin to live again. There will come a kind of inner happiness that no cloud of ill-fortune can dim.

I do not understand why it is that some of life's deepest insights and larger truths are ushered into our lives by pain and sorrow. I often feel like the little boy who wondered why God put the vitamins in spinach rather than in ice cream (where they ought to be). But I do know there is no such thing as a problem without a gift in its hand. It remains for us to unwrap the gift.

Sometimes the loveliest music is heard when adversity is at its height.

Many times through the years, I have thought of the legend of a baron who built his castle by the Rhine. From crag to crag and turret to turret, he hung wires, hoping that the winds blowing on this great harp might make sweet music. Long and patiently he waited, while around his castle winds from the four corners of heaven blew. But no music came.

But one night, there arose a great storm that tossed the Rhine to fury. The black sky was stabbed with lightning, the thunder roared, the earth trembled, and the winds shrieked madly. The baron went to the door of his great castle to view the terrifying scene. And there, suddenly, he heard the sound of music, like angels singing through the storm. His great harp of wires had come alive at last. The tempest had given it a soul.

The story is legend. The truth it seeks is wisdom. Again and again, we come to see that great lives sing most gloriously when assaulted by the winds of adversity.

❧

Unsung Heroes

OMETHING IN ALL of us yearns for heroes. It is, I think, inherent in the human spirit to look up to those who have captured our imagination by acts of caring and courage.

I am starting to wonder, though, if this may be an age devoid of heroes. After all, an age which boasts of investigative reporting, in which the most private aspects of life once discreetly overlooked now are deliberately exposed to public scrutiny, makes it tough to have heroes.

Even the greatest among us have fallen, often on their own pens. Encouraged by agents or publishers, who seem to feed parasitically on weaknesses and indiscretions, they have lowered themselves in "tell all" autobiographies that leave little to the imagination.

Honesty and candor are commendable qualities, but refuse belongs in alley trash cans. There is no real merit in making it the centerpiece of the table.

The feet of clay revealed in the lives of several prominent political and religious leaders in recent years have left us searching for heroes to match the giants of whom we read: Albert Schweitzer, Gandhi, Hellen Keller, Mother

Teresa, Einstein, Dr. Martin Luther King Jr., Dietrich Bonhoffer, and others. Alas, except for a few athletic and folk heroes, most of those who come to us emerge from the past. There are, however, bona fide heroes among us. We just need to look for them in different places.

Each week at the Washington Husky football games, I admire the huge squad that comes running onto the field. But I also feel for the two thirds of that squad who suffer the bruises of scrimmage against the varsity during the week. They practice hard, suit up for each Saturday's game, and yet they seldom, if ever, get to play.

That takes a certain kind of perseverance, and I admire those who stay with it. They receive no press or pats on the back for a game well played, but they are heroes, nonetheless. They are recognized on the campus of one major university in our country. Near the playing field is a statue of a football player bearing the inscription:

> *Dedicated to the subs:*
> *They never made the team,*
> *But they made the team.*

Other heroes I have been thinking of lately are the hostages still held in the Middle East, forgotten by many, now that the threat of war has moved their plight off the front pages of the paper. As far as I know, there are no stories of dramatic daring recorded in relation to their captivity, and I doubt whether they conform to the classic definition of heroism.

Why, then, consider them heroes? Because we see in them a characteristic of authentic heroism that may be more common and more important than some of the other attributes ordinarily associated with heroism. When there is nothing they can do, they nevertheless endure. In spite of adverse circumstances, loneliness, and despair, they have the strength and will to do all that can be done—they hang on. Sometimes it takes more courage just to live than it does to die.

I see another form of this special brand of heroism all around me, and I never cease to be lifted in spirit by those who stay with it, even though things are not what they wished they would be. Through the years I have known unheralded heroes and heroines who have forsaken their own plans and pleasures to care for an invalid spouse, parent, or child.

Their loyalty and tenderness are not publicized, but day by day they do the tasks at hand with cheerfulness and competence. They are the true saints of our world—people through whom the light does shine.

There are single parents who rise early, prepare breakfast for the family, leave children at day-care centers or school, work hard all day at the office, store, or classroom, return home late afternoon, prepare the evening meal, spend time with the children, wash, iron, and tend to a host of other details of the household—and then at a late hour fall, totally exhausted, into bed. Is this not heroism?

There are those who walk our streets who are veterans of mental health wards. They are battle-scarred and disabled in various ways. They are staging a difficult fight in the mental-health world. Nobody wants anything to do with them.

The government allocates relatively few dollars for their housing or medical treatments. They sleep in doorways and live on handouts. Their courage in facing the cold of both climate and human rejection is heroic. They do not rob or steal, nor are they violent or cruel, but they do their best to survive. To me, this is a high type of heroism.

There are those who didn't quite make it in the corporate race for the roses, yet they carry on in life's second places with undiminished optimism and courage. Others dwell in bodies of pain, twisted by deformity or disease and yet they stand tall in spirit and free of complaint.

There are those who dreamed great dreams for their children, only to see those dreams turn to heartaches, and yet they move among us with dignity and grace.

The world is not devoid of heroes and heroines, after all. I've only just begun. We see them around us every day. They will not capture the attention of the media often or be recipients of medals, but they deserve to be saluted for the staying power they reveal.

This article originally appeared November 3, 1990
in The Seattle Times.

✥

JULY

An America of Progress

O NE OF THE most dangerous evils in the world is the highly prized habit of always looking only on the bright side of things.

I would dislike having to live with anybody who habitually looked on the dark side, but it remains a most dangerous idea to suppose that, as a matter of course, everything will come out all right. Or one who believes it is a shining virtue to at least keep on saying that it will; that nice people can always see the silver lining in every cloud, and that God's in his heaven and all's right with the world.

This attitude is sheer sentimentality and there is no health in it. In fact, there is danger in it, for superficial optimists are a peril in serious times. An honest recognition of an ill is the first step toward its cure.

But somewhere between continual optimism and persistent despair is the happy working medium of reality.

It is easy to compile a list of negatives as we think about our nation. However, we never build up anything by continually tearing it down. To be fair, and to give a stronger base from which to work to right the wrongs and strengthen the weak places, we can recognize what we have that makes us strong. See the virtues, name them, and make them our own.

Beneath the threatening, deceptive surface, I see an America more right than wrong, more good than evil, and with far more reason to hope than to despair. Consider a few of the reasons for hope and reassurance:

We are a free society—a privilege we too easily forget. Jan Masaryk, Czechoslovakian statesman, once told an American audience; "Raised in liberty, most Americans accept their freedom as a matter of course. Sometimes it seems to me you free people don't realize what you've got ... You can wake up in the morning free to do as you choose, to read what you wish, to worship the way you please ..."

We are a united people—unity that comes not by chance, but that has been earned by the work and skill of great statesmen of our past. In 1787, Nathaniel Gorham, a delegate from Massachusetts, rose in the Constitutional Convention and said, "Can it be supposed that this vast country, including the Western Territory, will in 150 years remain one nation?" Obviously, he did not suppose that it would.

But now, two hundred years later, we are united. Fifty states woven together like Joseph's coat of many colors, yet a unified whole. A nation across which we are free to travel without fifty passports. Our unity was—and is—an achievement that had to be created, nurtured, and maintained.

Strong as we are militarily, America's real strength is not in armed might, but in the cultural variety and talent of our citizens, our natural resources, the democratic government that binds us together, and the religious foundation that has undergirded our nation since the earliest hour. Our successful yet continuing struggle to abolish prejudices in America is one of the giant steps to a human and moral civilization.

We are free to worship as we choose. Obscene distortions of religion and antiquated theologies are propagated from many pulpits, but thousands of churches and synagogues disseminate religious ideas that are both intellectually defensible and emotionally satisfying. Thousands of unheralded religious leaders, in quiet and unassuming ways, make ours a brighter, better, more loving nation.

Millions of men and women take their religious commitments seriously and translate faith into daily acts of love and caring for others. We take this for granted and notice only those who are spending money for an emotional jag or some form of so-called religious entertainment.

Millions of husbands and wives in our nation love each other devotedly and faithfully, and do not care to love another in the same way. But the high publicity goes to marital infidelities and the sordid stories that accompany them.

Despite seeming "evidence" to the contrary, Americans are among the most law-abiding citizens in the world. They pay their taxes, obey traffic rules, keep contracts, return lost property, and support statutes with a fidelity that is hard to match. It is precisely because so many people are honest that some can be dishonest. If dishonesty were the norm, every bank teller would be armed and each customer would be suspect.

Americans honor election returns. Political transitions are smooth and amicable. After the vote-counting come handshakes and pledges of support, not recriminations and bloodshed.

America has few deeper needs than for men and women who maintain undiscouragable hope and confidence in our country and its future. If we continually put down our nation, it will become too weak and shattered to rise to the challenge and possibilities it faces.

We are blessed by God to live in America in this tumultuous, difficult, but extraordinary age.

We have known much good, but the best is yet to be. On this Fourth of July, "Hats off to the past; rolled-up sleeves for the future."

Olympians in Our Midst

HE EYES OF millions will be centered on Barcelona, Spain, tomorrow through August 9, where nearly 11,000 athletes from 170 nations will be competing for supremacy in athletic skills. Such an assembly of well-conditioned, world-class performers captures our imagination.

Our fascination with star athletes is understandable because we love excellence born of discipline and hard work wherever we see it. I am among those who appreciate athletic skills, and yet I feel the adulation given to athletes often borders on idolatry and is out of the proportion to the importance of athletics.

This is especially true when, in idolizing those with athletic skills, we overlook others among us whose achievements are also great triumphs of the spirit. They, too deserve admiration and plaudits.

Perhaps what is needed in our world is an Olympics of the Spirit. Were such an event brought to pass, proficiency in various qualities of the spirit could be made known.

One category would be Resilience. The dictionary defines resilience as, "the power to return to original form or position after being bent, compressed, or stretched."

In the classification of resilience would be demonstrated the incredible capacity of people to bounce back after being "compressed, bent, or stretched."

Many wonderful people excel here. Gravely ill, they fight through to recovery and health. Phased out of one job, they train themselves for another. Separated and broken by divorce, they pull themselves together, avoid acute self-pity, and begin again, knowing that one chapter is not the whole of a book. Stung by the death of a cherished partner, they resume life alone, determined to find some joy in each day.

The classic testimony to resilience is offered by St. Paul in his second Corinthian letter, chapter four, verse eight: "We are afflicted in every way, but not crushed; perplexed, but not driven to despair; persecuted, but not forsaken; struck down, but not destroyed."

We salute the gymnasts of Olympic competition who spring across the mat with graceful agility and balance. But let us reserve our loudest cheers for the brave souls who, having fallen on darker days, have sprung back with remarkable resilience and recuperative power to meet life with faith and hope undiminished.

Initiative is the next category in the Olympics of the Spirit. Here, winners are those who have learned to stride into life with zest and confidence. They do not meet life on their heels, content only to counter the moves and blows of others. They act, not react.

Instead of cursing their genes, their parents, their circumstances, or their luck, they buck the negatives and assume responsibility for their own lives. They do not moan about how bad the world is. They take the initiative and work for the good it was intended to be.

Salute the Olympic boxers whose initiative enables them to carry the fight to their opponents, but let us reserve our highest commendation for those adventuresome spirits who refuse to be intimidated by difficult situations, take the initiative, and set out to bring good things to pass.

The power to Encourage is the third category in the Olympics of the Spirit. Encouragers serve in supportive roles. They have the God-inspired ability to get others started and keep them going.

They are cheerleaders, massaging the morale and enabling others to be better than they would otherwise be. This achievement may not stand out with high visibility, but it is an indispensable contribution to the success of all others who achieve.

Salute the Olympic weightlifters who press in excess of five hundred pounds, but let us express our deepest admiration and gratitude for those who lift others to their highest potential by their supportive love and encouragement.

Stamina is the final event. We are in the presence of gold-medal winners when we stand with older people who have the same enthusiasm and perseverance they had at an earlier age.

They answer the bell every morning. They are careful to groom themselves. They move out with purpose at home or on the job elsewhere. They manage to stay informed about the world. They mark out a sector for personal involvement.

They resist the shrill beckonings of current fads and fashions. They maintain a steady cheerfulness and confidence in God. They do not complain because they have ills—they are grateful that they have life.

Salute the marathon runner who covers twenty-six miles, but reserve the loudest cheers for the man or woman who stays with it against great odds in life and does not quit on the hills.

On such durable souls the cameras of heaven are trained. They shall not receive a perishable wreath, but the greatest prize of all: the Creator's "Well done!"

This article originally appeared July 25, 1992
in The Seattle Times.

The Influence of Affluence

MIDWESTERN NEWSPAPER sponsored a poetry contest which awarded prizes to the poets whose poems won the interest of most readers. One of the winning poems contained only two words: "Pay day."

Money never fails to capture the interest and imagination of all. Dorothy Parker said that the two most beautiful words in the English language are "check enclosed."

No one will question money's power and importance. The heaviest baggage to carry through life is an empty purse. The lack of money denies millions of people the amenities that make life worth living. Poverty condemns many to a squalid and incomplete existence.

Because money is of such value, it is easy to develop the desire to seek more of it. The yearning for more and more can lead to greed—a sin of such great dimension that the church fathers listed it among the seven deadly sins.

Greed is not new or unique to this generation. It is a continuing moral problem for each succeeding generation. The inordinate love of money and the habitual appeal of the money motive is present in nine-tenths of all the activities of life. The universal striving for economic security is the prime object of all endeavor, and the social approbation of money the prime measure of success.

A mystic from India was being introduced to New York City. His guide, with more nerve than wisdom, took him to the Times Square subway station at the peak morning rush hour. The visitor was appalled at what he saw—people with attaché cases pushing hard and driving madly. He could only think to ask, "Is there a wolf behind them?" "No," said the guide, "there's a dollar in front of them."

No one is immune to the insistent persuasion to acquire more. Enough is never quite enough. The drive for acquisitions works in a host of destructive ways.

Greed, which leads to excess, can blind us to the needs of those who have not.

It is possible to have so much power that we become indifferent to the rights and claims of others; to have so much health that we do not understand the sick or reckon with our own mortality; to have so many material goods that we prize possessions more than people, and worry into the night about losing what we have; to have so much knowledge that we become proud and self-sufficient.

Increasing wealth promises a more generous response in life that just does not materialize. Many find themselves under the influence of affluence. The more they have, the more reluctant they are to give. It is an illusion that when one reaches a certain income, the personal desires will be satisfied, leaving a larger margin for generosity. It just doesn't work that way. The more people accumulate, the more insatiable the appetite for even more.

People who know how much they are worth are often not worth that much. The real measure of our wealth is how much we would be worth if we lost all our money.

Philip Danforth Armour developed a family meat-packing business into the successful Armour and Company. Noting one day that the employees in a certain department of the company had increased their efficiency, Armour decided to present each of them with a new suit of clothes. He asked every man to order the suit of his choice and send the bill to Armour. One particularly greedy young man decided on a suit of evening clothes which cost considerably more than the others. Armour agreed to pay the bill, commenting to his clerk as he did so, "I've packed a great many hogs in my time, but I never dressed one before."

Those who give centrality to the acquisition of more and more of life's goods, to the neglect of human values, miss life's deepest joys and choicest riches.

Rudyard Kipling, during a commencement address at Montreal's McGill University, once said a striking thing that deserves to be remembered. Warning students against over-concern for money, position, or glory, he said, "Some day you will meet a person who cares for none of these things. Then you will know how poor you are."

A life devoted to the acquisition of wealth is useless unless we know how to turn it to joy. This is an art that requires culture, wisdom, and unselfishness.

In gratitude for God's goodness, and with responsibility for those less fortunate, sensible and caring people do not clamor for ever more of life's goods, but they share generously, and heed Gandhi's counsel—"Live simply that others may simply live."

Old-fashioned Sin

HERE IS AN old dialogue still making the rounds that goes like this:

"What did the minister preach about this morning?"

"He preached about sin."

"What did he say about it?"

"He was against it."

This, of course, is not so surprising. Ministers are supposed to be against sin. But my intent in this column is to reintroduce the recognition and admission of sin as a valid category in human experience, for the word "sin" has all but disappeared from today's thought and speech, and society has welcomed its disappearance.

It is certainly nothing new for men and women to refuse to acknowledge their sins, or to even think about them—they have been doing that since the earliest days of recorded history. But nowadays, we become elusive in a more sophisticated way, with glibness and with all sorts of euphemisms.

We speak of "error" and "transgression," of "infractions" and "mistakes," without admitting the accompanying exposure that goes with the serious use of that old-fashioned word, "sin."

Karl Menninger predicted this moral poverty in the mid 1970s when he wrote his prophetic book, *Whatever Became of Sin?* But now, a quarter-century later, in its first February issue this year, *Newsweek* featured the subject "Shame," with the subtitle, "How do we bring back a sense of right and wrong?"

True, this is a vital issue, and the loss of a sense of right and wrong in our country today is completely shameful and dangerous.

But sin does exist, and it cannot be so easily dismissed or left to the rescue missions, the itinerant evangelists, fundamentalist sects, and "Prepare to meet your God" road signs. It was Harry Emerson Fosdick, one of America's most liberal preachers, who said, "One of the chief perils of our time is a silly underestimate of the tremendous power of sin."

A priest who for years had listened to confessions of nuns was asked what it was like to have such an experience, week after week. He replied, with a twinkle in his eye, "It's like being stoned to death with popcorn." And it would, indeed, be difficult to imagine any great sins that certain people might commit.

But sins come in two categories: sins of commission and sins of omission. In our society, with all its possibilities and needs, many of us fail to do what we are able to do. We tend to think of sin only as something we have done.

When a consideration of ethics begins with issues such as dancing, Sunday movies, swearing, and the like, God's greater demands are humiliated by caricature. By burrowing into these and other small questions we can easily dismiss the large, and, in the process, miss our date with destiny.

The medieval church listed seven deadly sins: anger, pride, sloth, gluttony, envy, lust, and greed. How often and how seriously do we consider these sins in our personal lives today?

Much of modern religion is characterized by a jaunty sense of moral well-being. When we admit our sins, if we do so at all, we do it with complacency and even cheerfulness—"Our sins have been forgiven." And our religion often becomes an easy self-righteousness.

We cannot go against the grain of the universe without getting splinters. The mills of God grind slowly, but they grind exceedingly fine. "Be sure," says the Bible, "your sins will find you out."

Almost every issue of the daily newspaper reveals someone who has been "found out." One way or another, transgressions do come to light. And although God can forgive the sin, God cannot remove the consequences.

Ethical derelictions tend to blunt the perceptions. There comes a time when sin has so disintegrated the mental powers of the sinner that he or she no longer possesses the skill to conceal what ultimately cannot be hidden.

The person who stumbles, when first entering a sinful way is the lucky one, for then there is the opportunity to retreat from the path of destruction before habits become too strong to be broken. Otherwise, cobwebs soon become cables.

Sin makes a person careless. Those who sin year after year with apparent impunity often delude themselves into believing the path is clear and there is no danger of discovery. It is a generally accepted fact among students of criminology that even the most experienced criminals seem to eventually walk deliberately into captivity, having grown careless as the years pass without their being discovered.

Remorse and penitence are words that need to be brought back into our vocabularies. Science has demonstrated that humanity's greatest task is to triumph over those qualities we have in common with the beast of the jungle. The universe is not automatically progressing to perfection. Evil will never be eliminated by any gentle evolutionary process. Human salvation from sin is the central problem of the ages.

All the progress this world will ever know awaits the conquest of sin. Strange as it may sound to the ears of this modern age, long tickled by the amiable idiocies of belief in an easy-going God, our most critical need is for a fresh sense of personal and social sin, and the penitence and reform for which it calls.

Quiet Wounds

HEN WE LISTEN to a lecture or a sermon, attend an opera or see a play, we usually don't know what is going on in the lives of those who are sharing their talents with us.

Sometimes a performer, lecturer, or preacher is grieving, yet the speaker's courage is so great and the contribution so inspiring that those who listen are unaware that the one before them is suffering.

Beverly Sills, director of the New York City Opera, sang gloriously before capacity audiences in Metropolitan Opera productions when her heart was breaking because of her children's physical problems. Many times when she was not well herself, she went on stage and performed magnificently. She did not want to disappoint those who had come to hear her sing. Because she lost herself in the concert's demands, she was able to hide her pain.

She once was asked if she was a happy woman. Her answer was a perceptive and revealing one. "No," she said, "I am not a happy person, but I am a cheerful one. There is a difference. A happy person is one who has no cares. A cheerful person is one who has cares but tries to deal with them in constructive and positive ways."

Mark Twain lectured across Europe to earn enough money to pay huge debts from an unwise investment. Much of the time he was speaking, he was extremely tired and sickly, but he plodded on. His humor and wisdom were so captivating that his audiences had no idea Twain was troubled. When friends suggested that he could get out from under his debts by legal maneuvering, he refused to follow their advice saying, "Honor is a harder master than the Law."

This summer, thousands are again visiting the famed Passion Play at Oberammergau in Germany. The play dates to 1633, when the bubonic plague ravaged the Ammer Valley, killing eighty-five villagers in several months. Surviving residents made an oath to prepare and perform the play in ten-year intervals. This summer's performance marks the 350th anniversary of the oath.

In 1890, there was a tragedy within the tragedy. Every young man in the village hoped someday to be chosen for the part of Christus and every young girl yearned to play the Blessed Virgin Mary. In 1890, the young woman selected for the role was engaged to be married. Her betrothed insisted that the marriage take place that spring, and that she give up the chance to appear in the play.

She begged him to wait until autumn, explaining that to play Mary would glorify her whole life. The young peasant became very angry and told her she must choose between the play and him. She chose the play. His pride was greater than his love; he forsook her and made a hasty marriage.

All summer long she played the part of Mary, though

her own heart was pierced with sorrow. Thousands who attended throughout the summer were unaware of her heartache and loneliness. In the autumn of that year she entered a convent.

It is not only onstage that others conceal their sorrows from us. Often our closest friends experience disappointment, sorrow, and loss, but cloak their pain. The best actors and actresses are not in Hollywood, but nearby.

Ian MacLaren, a noted Scotsman, author of "Beside the Bonnie Brier Bush," cared deeply about those around him. His oft-quoted words offer wise counsel: "Be kind. Everyone you meet is carrying a heavy burden."

Ashleigh Brilliant elaborates on that philosophy by saying, "Be kind to unkind people: they probably need it most."

AUGUST

Passion & Patience

HAVE IN MY library a well-thumbed copy of John Bunyan's *Pilgrim's Progress*, which I read and re-read in the days when my favorite reading position was to lie on my stomach with my heels in the air. The picture in the book that fascinated me the most was that of the children, Passion and Patience.

I am compelled to confess that although Passion was supposed to be a wicked little rascal, he appealed to me more. There he sat, with flashing eyes, pouting mouth and clenched fists. Patience, on the other hand, wore an artificially angelic expression.

As I visualize the picture across the gulf of more than fifty years, I realize that it was the artist who gave poor little Patience that rather inane simper. The fault was not with Bunyan. Patience, however, is not mentioned as one of the virtues of medieval theology. In general, it is looked upon as a weak passivity rather than as one of the heroic virtues. Yet patience is a quality upon which harmonious, happy human relations absolutely depend.

A person who lacks patience can never hope to live peaceably with other human beings. Patience is the best of antidotes for touchiness, cantankerousness, and a super-acid disposition. Without it there cannot exist a social mind, a social heart, or a social will. Each of us has a special weakness which anyone who sees us at close range will discover sooner or later. We all make demands upon the patience of those who live with us and work with us.

That we all stand in need of patience makes it highly apparent that we should show it to others. It is wisdom and common sense to resolve to be tender with the young, compassionate with the aged, sympathetic with the striving, tolerant with the weak and erring, for sometime in life, we will have been all of these.

Impatience is often the sin of the talented. Highly gifted men and women are sometimes impatient with those whose mental processes are slower. But to praise the person with great gifts and laugh at one with small is a particularly loathsome trait. Often our laughter is tinged with contempt. And contempt is a source of alienation.

Patience is not as commonplace a characteristic as it appears to the superficial observer. Virtues and vices do not exist in separated compartments of life. For example, tolerance and patience walk hand in hand. The man without sympathy is never patient.

Impatience and irritability are almost synonymous. Arrogance and selfishness are responsible for much of the impatience by which people persecute their dependents and associates.

Today, Patience is indeed a Virtue. We all have need of much of it, for without it, we are failures as human beings.

Room for Keepsakes

I HAVE TWO FRIENDS who are facing that perplexing dilemma of moving from a large, well-furnished home to a condominium. Theirs has been a lifetime of collecting and saving every conceivable item.

Although they have given many things to their children and to charities, they still have drawers, closets, and a garage full of more items than can be accommodated in their small quarters.

The things we collect and save through the years have value for us. Clothes, letters, pictures, household items, and furniture represent extensions of our own personalities. It is understandable that we part with them reluctantly.

Keepsakes we have either purchased or received as gifts enrich our lives. They lighten the darkening halls of memory, keeping alive experiences and associations that define who we are.

Keepsakes can be invaluable gifts to our children, grandchildren, or young friends who live after us. They bring a bond with the past that strengthens and gives meaning to our personal lives.

They can also strengthen society. We are not entire in

ourselves. Our ancestors, families, and friends are the rest of us.

I empathize with friends who are now determining what must be given away or sold. I have been through this process myself.

When I pondered this problem, my mind took flight. I began to think of collections we can make with which we do not have to part, no matter how limited our living quarters become. I am thinking now of the collectibles that are intangible but nonetheless real.

If we have a collector's eye, we will find all sorts of things to collect: stars moving majestically through the dark of night, tall grasses shimmering in the sun, clouds moving across the heavens, white sails silhouetted against a blue sky, Mount Rainier catching the last rays of the evening sun.

There is a wealth of beauty around us each day just waiting to be collected. How sad when we pass sightless and unheeding. Wordsworth collected precious memories when he saw a field of golden daffodils:

> *For oft when on my couch I lie*
> *In vacant or in pensive mood,*
> *They flash upon that inward eye*
> *Which is the bliss of solitude*
> *And then my heart with pleasure fills*
> *And dances with the daffodils.*

Try collecting smiles. You will be so pleased with your collection you will want to keep right on collecting.

Of course, you have to smile first. Start with the first person you see and continue throughout the day.

There are times people will not return your smile. They may be wondering why you are smiling, or they may be tired, worried, preoccupied, or ill. Or they may be surprised!

> *The world is like a mirror*
> *Reflecting what you do*
> *If you smile right out at others*
> *They'll smile right back at you.*

Emily Dickinson expressed another reason for her smile:

> *They might not need me*
> *Yet they might.*
> *I'll let my face be just in sight*
> *A smile as small as mine might be*
> *Precisely their necessity!*

If you keep right on trying, sooner or later you'll get some kind of a smile for your collection. Often the one that's hardest to get is the one you'll prize the most.

Collect some sound each day. It could be the soft lap of waves or the bubbling laughter of a child. It might be the high, clear sound of a bird or symphony of insect sounds.

Sort out the beautiful sounds. Select sounds that soothe the spirit and quiet the nerves. Listen often to great music and find that the melody lingers afterward.

Close your eyes and listen carefully. You can often hear the cries of people who are hurting. Let it be a call for you to help. Collect and memorize one beautiful thought each day. It might be a verse of scripture, a stanza of poetry, or a word of wisdom.

It may be the thoughtful encouraging word of a friend. Let the walls of your mind become a picture gallery that can be carried with you wherever you are, or into whatever house you move. We do not often lose what we once knew. What we learn can settle into the subconscious to become the reservoir from which we draw our responses to life.

> *The tide recedes but leaves behind*
> *bright seashells on the sand,*
> *The sun goes down, but gentle warmth*
> *still lingers on the land,*
> *The music stops, and yet it echoes on*
> *in sweet refrains ...*
> *For every joy that passes,*
> *something beautiful remains.*

> *—Hadin Marshall*

A Greater Mission

TWO VERY IMPORTANT days in every life are the day we are born and the day when we know why we were born. But there are many, living and dead, who never experience that second day. For it is as Isaac Watts once wrote:

> Most people creep into the world
> And know no reason why they are born
> Except to consume the corn and fish
> And leave behind an empty dish.

It is a pity if a person comes to the time when he must die only to discover that he never really lived. Methodist Bishop Gerald Kennedy has described the most tragic kind of a funeral service a minister is called upon to conduct.

"It is not," said the wise bishop, "the kind that would seem obviously to be tragic. It is not the service for a youth whose life has been snuffed out before he has even reached maturity, nor is it for the infant who never gets a chance at living. Rather, it is for those who have never learned to live—who come to their final hours with no friends, and have contributed nothing with the time and talents entrusted to them."

It is normal to desire meaning for our lives. This need is reflected vividly in thoughts that often afflict people in middle or later years as they look back. Did I waste my life? Did I give what was in me to give? Have I climbed the ladder of success only to find it was leaning against the wrong wall?

I have listened many times to men and women experiencing those second thoughts, the aching regrets over mistakes or lost opportunities which can't be corrected or relived. John Gardner, founder of Common Cause, tells of a friend who asks the same question of almost every new acquaintance, "What have you done that you believe in and are proud of?"

Obviously, it is an unsettling question for people who have built their esteem on their wealth or their family name or an exalted job title. The old fellow is not being cantankerous, nor is it his intent to put people down. "I really don't care how they answer," he said. "I just want to put the thought in their minds. They should live their lives in such a way that they have a good answer. Not a good answer for me—for themselves. That is important."

Everyone has noticed the enthusiasm and tenacity of purpose exhibited by people who believe in what they are doing. It is as though they had tapped some inexhaustible underground reservoir of energy. But the absolute necessity is to discover something that lifts us out of ourselves to what Reinhold Niebuhr called a more ultimate majesty than that of our own pride, a more ultimate center of life than that of our own construction.

William Menninger (Karl's brother), a brilliant psychiatrist in his own right and a devoted Christian, toured the country for years as a lecturer and consultant. He was frequently asked the secret of a good, happy, and useful life. His answer was usually the same: "Find a worthwhile mission in life and take it seriously."

The commitments that people make to values beyond themselves are manifested in various ways—in their family life, their community life, their religious life, in the standards they set for themselves, and in the way they treat any and all humans.

People can achieve meaning in their lives only if they have made commitments to the development of their own highest possibilities, commitments to loved ones and to all humanity, and a commitment to the divine power beyond themselves. Our great American philosopher, William James, summed it up in one sentence. "The great use of life is to spend it, for something that outlasts it."

The Pursuit of Happiness

NE OF THE modern myths that persists in our society is that every person has the right to expect a life of continuing happiness. We live with the assumption that there is something in our very nature that correctly claims our right to such a state.

So when we are happy, we accept our condition as being our right, and when we are not happy, we complain and protest an unfair infringement on the "right" we believe to be inherent.

In this concept we deliberately set the stage for our own discontent. In expecting happiness as a firm right, we set the very conditions for creating unhappiness in our lives. When we expect life to be one fun-filled experience after another, we learn that life is not always fun-filled.

If we adopt the "pleasure principle" as a rule of life, we soon discover that life is a tightly woven tapestry of both the pleasant and the unpleasant. All is not velvet. Some is sandpaper. It is the beginning of wisdom when we recognize this. When we accept that much of life is hard, it somehow becomes amazingly easier—easier for us, and for those around us who are spared our complaints.

Sometimes we pay a great price for our wholly unrealistic expectations. At the first sign a marriage may not be perfect after all and might not qualify for the "made in heaven" label, there can come too often an early disintegration of the relationship and turn toward divorce. Most marriages are not made in heaven. They come in kits, and we must put them together ourselves.

When the fresh idealism of a newly launched professional career is struck by the inescapable discords of reality, premature disillusionment can set in. Someone should tell us at that early date that success comes to no one. We must go to success, and the journey is often not easy.

An ambitious young man approached a successful businessman with "Please tell me the secret of your success."

"There is no easy secret," was the reply. "You must jump at every opportunity."

"But how can I know when my opportunity comes?" the young man asked. The businessman replied, "You can't. You have to keep jumping."

The hard truth is that we have no right to happiness, per se. Life carries no such warranty. The recognized right in our Constitution is the *pursuit* of happiness—a procedure that may be unrewarding and carry with it some risks. Those who set out to pursue happiness seldom find it. (To understand this is to avoid the pain of self-inflicted unhappiness.) For happiness is not a product to be found but a byproduct of the search.

We do not discover happiness through an unrelenting pursuit of it. Happiness comes from within, welling up from the quiet and deep recesses of the heart. Its strength and inner peace is something quite apart from the external factors of our existence.

The highest prospect for happiness comes to those who strive to do the Creator's will to serve rather than to be served. Happiness is not their goal in life. Character is. True happiness involves the full use of one's powers and talents. Happiness comes when we know that we do not necessarily require happiness. It is not the fulfillment of what we want but the realization of the goods we already have.

In such a response to life, many of the anxieties about rewards and recognition disappear, petty insults and criticisms lose their sting, and rivalries, comparisons, and envies vanish. The happiness that comes was not initially sought, but is the interest received for the investment in a life of love and helpfulness.

> *Go not abroad for happiness.*
> *For see,*
> *It is a flower that blooms at thy door.*
> *Bring love and justice home,*
> *and then no more*
> *Thou'lt wonder in what dwelling*
> *Joy may be.*
>
> *—Minot J. Savage*

Learning the Lesson of Peace

IFTY YEARS AGO, August 6, 1945, at 8:15 in the morning, on a clear, cloudless day, came the event that changed the face of the future: the first atomic bomb was dropped on Hiroshima.

Much has happened in the years since that day, and life with the bomb seems often to have lost its reality. But the bomb and its related atomic weaponry still rule our world.

Many wish the day had never happened, and some, in their wishing, tend to try to bury it. For many Americans, fifty years is a long time ago, and Hiroshima is far away. But I remember it clearly today because of an experience I had thirty-four years ago.

In the late summer of 1960, I received a letter from the leaders of the United Church of Japan, inviting me to join thirteen other American Protestant ministers from across the country in a mission to Japan to work with Christian churches and their leaders there in the summer of 1961.

The fourteen of us in the program were placed in different cities and parishes in Japan. My assignment for the summer was to work with Kenji Takakura and his wife, Tazuko, who were ministers in a mission in the rag-pickers' district, a slum area in Tokyo.

Mineo Goto, a student at International Christian University in Tokyo, was assigned as my companion and interpreter. It was a joy and a privilege to work with these fine young people.

The mission was in the Fukagawa section of the city, near Tokyo Bay. It was an area of flimsy shacks and shelters, factories and apartments, where thousands of poverty-stricken people did their best to survive. It was an area that had been demolished by American incendiary bombs in May of 1945, when one hundred thousand people were cremated by the fires. The boiling waters of the canals had offered no refuge.

It was a busy and eventful summer of work in the mission and schools in the surrounding area, but it remained for the final days of the summer to provide the most sobering and memorable experience of all.

It was then that Kenji, Tazuko, Mineo, and I traveled the 554 miles to Hiroshima to deliver gifts to patients at the hospital where atomic bomb victims were being cared for.

We were welcomed by Dr. Fumio Shigeto, the chief administrator at the hospital, a physician who was a victim of the bomb. He answered our questions and told us of the suffering and pain that still persisted in Hiroshima sixteen years after the bomb.

We saw some of it firsthand when we visited in many rooms of the large hospital and talked with the people who had been bedridden since the bomb fell.

Many of those with whom we visited requested prayer and offered thanks for our visit, for theirs was a lonely and sad existence, and visitors were few. (How easy to remember the staggering statistics of thousands killed by the explosion, yet how quickly we forget the aftermath of such devastation.)

I remember especially my conversation with one of the patients—a highly intelligent woman in her thirties, a teenager when the bomb fell. Her body was badly scarred, and she had no legs.

"Mr. Turner," she said, "we do not feel sorry for ourselves. Thousands did not survive at all. But if only we could believe that our suffering is not in vain, and that it would mean the end of nuclear war, then we would gladly bear our pain on behalf of the world.

"It would have some redemptive value. But we have news of an arms build-up in many places of our world, and the hope of lasting peace becomes ever more dim."

We assume that the whole world does want peace. But, of course, that is not true. People who experience no genuine satisfaction in life do not want peace. Men court war to escape meaninglessness and boredom, to be relieved of fear and frustration. And peace does allude us because, unfortunately, we do not give peace the priority it deserves.

In his book, *Human Options*, Norman Cousins wrote:

> Our knowledge is vast but does not embrace the working of peace. Because we attach importance to a rounded view of life, we study history, philosophy, religions, language, literature, art, architecture, and political science.
>
> Because we are concerned about our well-being, we study anthropology, biology, medicine, psychology, and sanitation. Because we are interested in technical

progress, we study chemistry, physics, and engineering. But we have yet to make the making of peace central to our education.

We miss an important lesson of history when we fail to realize that the easiest way for any nation to destroy itself is to make national security the highest value.

People are never more insecure than when they become obsessed with their fears at the expense of their dreams, or when the ability to fight becomes more important than the things worth fighting for.

We can govern the atomic bomb if we will. Thomas Edison said, "What man's mind can create, man's character can control."

There are many prayers with which to begin each new day. At this memorable time, and on every day, let us pray again: "Let there be peace on Earth, and let it begin with me."

This article originally appeared on August 5, 1995
in The Seattle Times.

SEPTEMBER

Dignity of Labor

ABOR DAY WEEKEND is a good time to reflect on work and its place in our daily lives.

Many would not list work among their favorite words, yet the ability and opportunity to work are among God's greatest gifts. One has only to be unemployed or forced to remain idle to discover how debilitating it can be to have nothing to do.

Michelangelo, the great Italian sculptor and architect, once said, "It is only well with me when I have a chisel in hand."

Dr. Charles Mayo kept a motto on the wall of his office. "There is no fun like work."

Still, no matter how enjoyable an occupation may be, some days are nothing but drudgery and monotony, and we must drive ourselves to get work done.

Dr. Charles Eliot, former president of Harvard, confessed many years after assuming leadership of the university that his job no longer offered him either novelty or fresh interest. He went so far as to say that nine-tenths of it had become sheer routine—as dull and monotonous to him as the work of carpenters or blacksmiths was to them.

It is exactly because work can be a bore that religious bodies have continuing responsibility to make clear the relationship between faith and daily toil.

Faith can be nurtured in work. The highest reward for toil is not what we get for it, but what we become by it. It is in our work that our integrity is revealed. The test of a man's religion is not only the way he gives his money, but the manner in which he earns it.

What, after all, is the meaning of religious commitment if at the very center of a man's life he defrauds his neighbor with dishonest dealings or insults God with shabby craftsmanship? No amount of piety on the Sabbath can atone for a crooked deal on Wednesday. Sunday is not a sponge intended to wipe out the sins of the week.

In fact, an Eleventh Commandment is in order: "Remember the Weekday to Keep it Holy." Because people spend most of their week in schools, homes, offices, and factories, God is as interested in them as he is in churches.

He is not so interested in what job a person does. At one time, societies classified vocations and professions as though some were holier than others. This is sheer nonsense—a medieval heresy that persists in the minds of many.

It is time we are through with the narrow view that a man is doing religious work only when he is preaching a sermon, teaching a Bible class, ushering, serving on a church board, singing in a choir, or preparing a church dinner. These are sacred and needed services, but they are not more sacred than preparing a meal for a family, washing a dish, being a fair employer or a faithful employee, teaching in a public or private school, or helping in any one of the hundreds of ways that people serve to meet human need.

A man is just as religious whether he makes soap or sermons, practices preaching or plumbing—provided there is character and integrity in both.

It is a fallacious prejudice that ascribes dignity to briefcases, white collars, and academic robes, while denying it to lunch pails, muddy overalls, and greasy caps.

Pat, a hod carrier on a building project, was visiting with his foreman. "Didn't you tell me," he asked Pat, "that your brother is a bishop?"

"Indeed he is," said Pat.

"And you a hod carrier—well, your talents were certainly divided unevenly."

"They surely were," replied Pat. "My brother couldn't do this to save his life!"

It will be a great day when services of ordination are held for hod carriers and all other laborers who do useful work with faithfulness and honesty. Theirs, too, is a contribution to the substance of the universal good as the most brilliant "professional," the most compelling preacher.

※

Learning to Love

ITH THE ARRIVAL of September, the classrooms of our nation are opened and the educational process begins anew. I was intrigued by a comment relating to education made by the famous anthropologist, Ashley Montagu. He writes that the main purpose of education is the art and science of being a warm and loving human being.

"It could be argued," he contended, "that our education is a failure, no matter what it has done for our head, if it has done little or nothing for our heart."

Montagu's comment is obviously an overstatement to make a point. Education must be concerned with the development of competence and expertise in many vocations and professions. But it cannot be denied that all life and all work is enhanced and glorified when infused with a loving spirit.

The healthiest and most completely whole and creative human beings are those who know and practice what it is to give love in non-demanding, non-manipulative ways. Love is the active power which enables us to break through walls that separate us—the doorway through which the

human spirit moves from solitude to society, from selfishness to service.

Love permits us to overcome the sense of isolation and
separateness which often engulfs us, and yet it permits us
to be ourselves.

Dr. Erich Fromm wrote more than thirty books, many
of them dealing with love. Fromm wrote, "People believe
that nothing is easier than to love, but on the contrary, while
every human being has the capacity for love, its realization
is one of the most difficult achievements."

However, although the expression of love is sometimes
difficult, it is not impossible. There are at least four simple
ways to begin —ways that are within the range of all of us.

The first duty of love is to listen. To listen to another is
to affirm that person, and to enhance his or her sense of
self-worth. In his book, *Love Against Hate*, Dr. Karl
Menninger says, "Listening is a magnetic and strange
thing—a creative force. The friends who listen to us are the
ones we move toward, and we want to sit in their radius.
When we are listened to, it creates us, makes us unfold and
expand." Becoming an attentive and empathetic listener is
possible for all of us. We do not have to be wealthy, schol-
arly, or talented to give this gift.

> *His thoughts were slow*
> *His words were few*
> *And never formed to glisten*
> *But he was a joy to all his friends*
> *You ought to have seen him listen.*

The second duty of love is to see the good in others. In
most people, love is not absent, it is merely undiscovered.

Many people do not know how beautiful they can be. They need to be given hints. "Love is blind" is a proverb that expresses only half of the truth. Love is the only reality that truly sees.

It calls into being what is sometimes hidden from the sight of the uncaring or superficial observer. Before Jesus taught his disciples, he loved them. He was not unaware of their weaknesses, but he appealed to their strengths. Several centuries later, Saint Augustine, reflecting Jesus' spirit, said, "Dig deep enough into anyone and you will find something divine."

The third duty of love is to say something to affirm the love that is felt. There is a shortage in our day of genuine, heartfelt appreciation. There are critics by the hundreds, but the person who takes the time and trouble to mention the commendable is all too rare. The poet George Eliot (Mary Ann Evans) said, "I do not want only to be loved, but to be told that I am loved. The realm of silence is large enough beyond the grave."

The fourth duty of love is to do something for someone else each day at some cost to ourselves. Some people talk so much about what they intend to do that there is no time left after all the talking is through.

Dr. Charles Mayo was not only a great medical doctor, but he was an equally great human being. He had what he called a "flowers for the living" philosophy.

Over and over again in his classrooms, he reminded his students that, "An ounce of taffy is better than a pound of epitaphy." One genuine tear of compassion shed for the living is better than a faceful of tears for the dead. The smallest good deed is better than the grandest good intention.

These are simple expressions of love, but I present them to you as at least a place to start.

> *A bell is no bell till you ring it*
> *A song is no song till you sing it*
> *Love in the heart wasn't put there to stay*
> *Love isn't love till you give it away.*

Hate, Like Acid, Burns from Within

HE PICTURE OF Yitzhak Rabin and Yasser Arafat shaking hands in Washington, D.C., on September 13, 1993, will be etched in our minds for a long time to come. Who would have believed it!

But we rejoice in it. It was an important step toward ending bloodshed and bringing peace to the Middle East. Much remains to be done, but it is a beginning.

All efforts toward oneness and human accord are welcomed. The deepest need of the human spirit is community—common unity—good will and acceptance. Alienation, estrangement and ill will are contrary to God's will and the best interests of the human family.

One of the most frightening aspects of human conduct is the length nations and individuals will go to keep offenses alive.

They will massage them. They will give them artificial respiration, trying to pump life into them, and will breathe fresh anger, irritation, and resentment into them long after the original offense is gone and its pulse has stopped. They will not let dead deeds rest.

This is sad, for revenge degrades all who tolerate its

presence in their minds and hearts. A vengeful spirit should be condemned not only because it can lead to harming the offender, but because it also harms the one who harbors the grudge.

Clinical findings affirm that inner tensions can precipitate serious health crises as often as do organic diseases.

Malice, grudges, dwelling on past slights, cruelties, and injustices are among the tensions that often cause or worsen high blood pressure, heart disorders, and ulcers. "It isn't what we eat, but what's eating us that does the damage," the saying goes.

Enmity, hatred, and vindictiveness are like acid. They can do as much or more harm to the vessel in which they are stored as to that on which they are poured.

Jesus gave high priority to the kingdom of right relationships. He said, "So when you are offering your gift at the altar, if you remember that your brother or sister has something against you, leave your gift there before the altar and go; first be reconciled to your brother or sister, and then come and offer your gift." (Matthew 5:23-24)

There are constructive and common-sense ways to dissolve vindictiveness and enmity. Dale Carnegie said, "The best way to knock a chip off of another's shoulder is to give him a pat on the back."

This is basically true, but it can be false if it is done dishonestly only to gain a selfish advantage. Compliments are helpful if they are deserved. But integrity is violated if they are not sincere.

In human relationships, memory is an asset, but forgetfulness can be useful, as well. Toward the end of his life, Edward Everett Hale said, "I do not think that anybody ever had so many friends as I have had. However, I once had an enemy, a determined enemy, and I have been trying all day to remember his name."

The year after Benjamin Franklin was appointed clerk of the General Assembly, a member made a speech against him. Franklin did not embarrass the speaker by answering him on the floor of the assembly, although Franklin's keen mind and ready wit could have withered the man.

Instead, Franklin wrote his opponent, asking to borrow a certain book.

When the gentleman sent the book, Franklin wrote a warm letter of appreciation. After this exchange the two men began to visit one another and soon became good friends.

This was Benjamin Franklin's way of expressing good will. Since at the onset there had been no favor Franklin could do for his antagonist, he asked a favor of him, thus opening the gates of communication between them.

Franklin blessed his enemy with the assurance that an unfriendly act had not hopelessly divided them.

It is good common sense to end differences at an early hour. We never know when it will be to late to do so.

William Makepeace Thackeray and Charles Dickens, both eminent authors, had been estranged for a long period. One day they came within sight of one another in the Athenium Club of London.

Thackeray strode across the room to grasp Dickens' hand. "Shake hands with me. We are friends who cannot go on loving like this. Let us make peace."

The frostiness left Dickens' face. They were reconciled. Two days later Thackeray said, "How I love that fellow. I am happy to be reunited." Five days later, Thackeray was dead.

We are never so strong as when we forgo the desire for revenge and willingly forgive an injury. Booker T. Washington, the great black leader of Tuskegee Institute, was imbued with such a spirit.

Washington was treated rudely on several occasions by one of the citizens of Tuskegee, Alabama, but he always responded kindly to the offender.

A friend said to Washington, "Why do you continue being so polite to him when he is so sullen and rejecting of you?"

The great leader and educator responded, "I have no ill feeling toward him, and why should I let him determine how I shall act?" It is wise and magnanimous to never let any critical word or malevolent act maneuver us out of the orbit of unconditional love, acceptance, and good will.

Four lines by Edwin Markham convey a world of wisdom:

> *He drew a circle that shut me out*
> *Heretic, rebel, a thing to flout.*
> *But love and I had the wit to win:*
> *We drew a circle that took him in.*

ॐ

True Friendship

WANT TO WRITE a word about friendship. Surely, true friendship is a treasure to be valued beyond price. It cannot be bought, for if it is tendered because of what one person can do for another, it is unworthy of the name.

True friendship is not a matter of "connections." That grossly impersonal word is all too common in thought and speech. It is not a relationship forged for self-serving purposes. To maneuver or manipulate another person under the guise of friendship is frightfully demeaning and disgraceful. It is shamefully selfish. It is hypocritical camouflage abusing the true meaning of friendship.

Of course, when the testing-time for such so called "friendship" comes, that which was erroneously called "friendship" is seen for what it is: an acquaintance that lasted just as long as it served selfish purposes—and not a minute longer.

Next to family relationships, true friendship is marvelously enriching and a wonderfully supportive force in a person's life. Friendship makes it possible for a person to be open and honest, wholly without pretense. In friendship, you can allow yourself to be vulnerable; for a friend will accept you and your weaknesses, taking you just as you are. Whatever mask a person may wear in superficial relationships, protecting oneself from the possibility of misunderstanding or hurt, that mask may be removed before a true friend.

I like the way George Eliot marked this truth:

Oh, the comfort, the inexpressible comfort of feeling safe with a person; having neither to weigh thoughts nor measure words, but to pour them all out just as they are, chaff and grain together, knowing that a faithful hand will take and sift them, keeping what is worth keeping, and, then, with a breath of kindness, blow the rest away.

Furthermore, it is a virtue of true friendship that has the power to bring the best out of us. Somehow, one's own self-image is enhanced and made better through the trust of a friend. When a friend thinks kindly of us—often beyond what we feel is deserved—we want nothing more than to be worthy of that thought.

If one sees any good in us we earnestly want that good to become reality. If one trusts us, we will go to great ends to justify that trust. In this sense, friends are always involved in the process of making all of us what we are and what we shall be.

Elizabeth Barrett Browning asked of Charles Kingsley, one of England's greatest clergymen and novelists, "What is the secret of your life? Tell me, that I may make mine beautiful, too." Kingsley's simple reply was, "I had a friend."

Emerson's essay on friendship deserves reading and rereading. A sentence from that essay had stayed with me since college days: "The glory of friendship is not the out-stretched hand, nor the kindly smile nor the joy of companionship; it is the spiritual inspiration that comes to one when he discovers that someone else believes in him and is willing to trust him with his friendship."

True friends come in when the whole world has gone out. They are faithful to the very end. Leslie D. Weatherhead tells of two soldiers who became fast friends during World War I. When, after an unsuccessful night sortie, one of them was missing, the second youth heard a cry from no man's land. Reluctantly, the commanding officer granted permission for a rescue attempt, but added, "It's not worth it. Your friend is probably dead by this time. You will throw your life away."

The attempt was immediately made. When, some time later, the rescuer returned, he was dragging the body of his dead comrade. He himself was mortally wounded. Looking up at his commanding officer, he said with joy: "Sir, it was worth it. When I reached him, he looked up and said to me, 'I knew you'd come.'"

Hues of Courage

OURAGE WAS ONE of the first character traits to gain the admiration of the human race. The welfare of the community, its food supply, and clothing, indeed its very survival, depended directly upon the willingness of tribesmen to risk great peril in hunting and in war. Physical courage, therefore, was common, and absolutely necessary.

In modern times physical courage is less a daily requirement for most people. Hunting is more of a recreation than a requisite for survival. And most people are not directly engaged in combat. What happens to courage then, when occasions for its use diminish? Does it atrophy and finally disappear?

The need for courage is as great as ever, but in our time moral courage is demanded more often than physical courage.

Those who aim to live courageously today must often be willing to sacrifice momentary satisfactions and endure relative hardships for the sake of worthy goals and high causes.

Courage is not merely one of many virtues. An element

of courage can often be present in other virtues at the moment of testing.

Courage can be defined in many ways. It is standing by a conviction when no one else will stand with you. It is standing firm for truth and justice when peer pressures to opposing action are strong. Courage is the willingness to admit error and alter belief when new information leads to new truth. Courage is facing life anew when separation or divorce forces a redirection of early dreams and plans. Courage is coming home to an empty house with faith and hope after a loved one has been laid to rest.

Courage is standing by, caring for a family member who is ill for a long time when the caretaker is also often tired or ill. Courage is restraint when the temptation is strong to give in to physical desires. Courage is unselfish giving to another's desperate need when all that one has seems barely enough to live on. Courage is mercy and forgiveness when revenge would be sweet and timely and "would teach the other fellow a lesson." Courage is the willingness to break away when necessary from pleasant security and venture into the risky unknown.

Sometimes an ordinary experience can contribute to a courageous response. One aspiring writer who was afraid to marry his fiancee because his financial future was not assured, and who was reluctant to undertake a writing career because he feared failure, confessed he was given courage while watching a squirrel.

Sitting in a park, worrying about his prospects in life, the young man looked up to see a squirrel leaping from tree to tree. Once the little animal missed the limb he aimed for and fell, but caught himself on a lower limb. Then he leaped again and again until he arrived at his goal.

An old man sitting beside the writer remarked that he had watched many squirrels swinging from one leafy trapeze to another. He has seen many miss a limb, but always they caught another hold and only seldom was one hurt trying.

Then the aged philosopher chuckled and said, "I reckon you've got to take some risks if you don't want to spend all your life in one tree."

Two weeks later the young man married the girl and launched his writing career in earnest, and he always remembered the squirrel.

Courage is persistence despite discouragement.

Thomas Carlyle spent years researching and writing his history of the French Revolution. Before he took his finished work to the publisher, he loaned the manuscript to his friend and neighbor, John Stuart Mill.

Several days elapsed and Mill did not return the manuscript. At last he came to Carlyle's door, pale and trembling, and confessed that his housekeeper had carelessly used the manuscript to start a fire.

For many days Carlyle was alternately frenzied with anger and hopeless with despair. Years of hard labor had been utterly wasted. He was convinced he could never bring himself to write another line of history.

But one day while out walking, he stopped to watch a mason building a brick wall. The man laid only one brick at a time, but still the wall was raising toward completion.

Although Carlyle had thought he did not have the heart to write another book, he did resolve to write one page at a time and so page by page, his magnificent work on the

French Revolution was completed.

The courageous are not free from despair, but they struggle on.

We need courage not only to face life's big tests, but the small ones, as well. It takes courage to follow a regular routine, to stick to our plans, to keep petty irritations of the day from blocking efforts, and to keep on going, hour after hour. We need to remember that it isn't the big trees that trip us up as we walk through the forest, but the little vines on the ground—the exposed roots and low underbrush.

Courage is the conquest of fear, rather than the absence of it. Courage implies knowing the dangers, weighing them carefully, and then doing one's best, with God's help, to fulfill an important mission in the world, despite the dangers.

In a world that blazons "Safety First," the brave place God's will first. This is the highest courage of all—and the greatest wisdom.

❧

OCTOBER

A Time to Give

EVERAL DAYS AGO, I was leaving University Village in my car when I saw a young woman standing at the exit of the Village. She held a large sign that read: "Help me find a place to live and provide food for my two boys."

I drove on to my study, sat down and began to do the things I had scheduled for that day. And then, I began to have feelings of guilt. Why, I asked myself, did I not at least stop and inquire more about her need? Did I make a quick negative judgment about the validity of her professed poverty to salve my own conscience?

Why did I not give her what money I could and alert her to agencies that I know provide food and shelter?

I thought of the New Testament story of Dives, the rich man who fared sumptuously each day but was oblivious to Lazarus, the beggar who sat hungry at his gate. My feelings of guilt were accentuated by the memories of my childhood home and the lessons of sharing that my parents hoped I would learn.

When I was young, our home was near railroad tracks, where many freight and passenger trains were constant companions—as were the transients who rode the rails.

We often thought our house was marked in some way by those transients—hobos we called them then—for hardly a week went by that one or more of them didn't knock on our door, asking for food. It was a practice of my mother and dad never to turn anyone away hungry. One of the earliest memories of my childhood was of sitting on the porch of our home with grimy, hungry men who were feasting on the food my mother prepared for them.

With all of this working in my mind, I could no longer remain in my office, so I got into my car and drove back to visit with the young woman at the Village exit. But she was gone, and I had missed my call to help.

It was, of course, not an isolated or unique plea for assistance. The poor, the hungry, and the homeless confront us often. We see them sleeping on sidewalks, in doorways, and on park benches. And sometimes we meet them on street corners, begging for a few coins.

Their numbers are growing. On any given night, an estimated 735,000 people in the United States are homeless. At least two million may be without shelter for one night or more during the year. Statistics further reveal that as many as five million children in our country go to bed hungry each night.

Linda Stone, coordinator of the Governor's Task Force on Hunger in Washington state, pointed out that hungry children suffer more health problems than other children. Bread is basic.

In parts of India, in many African countries, and in other places of our world where hunger and poverty are continuous, American tourists are warned by tour guides to avoid beggars. Should neglect be our response to poverty, homelessness, and hunger at home as well?

Shall we pass our own countrymen, heedless and unseeing or uncaring? How do we relate to the staggering needs of our own nation?

"We must do something" will always solve more problems than "something must be done." So, what do we do?

We can care. Anyone who looks out at the world through dry eyes is not as compassionate as a person ought to be. There are those who do not care what happens as long as it doesn't happen to them. Caring is at least the initial form of helping.

We can have a lovers' quarrel with our nation. We can appreciate the good things America provides for our own citizens and for those of other lands. But we can be angered by our country's budget priorities—a budget that allows a pitifully small proportion of money for meeting the needs of the hungry and dispossessed.

In spending billions of dollars for guns, bullets, and technologically advanced weapons systems, and little for butter, bread, and housing for the poor, our budget allocations are a national disgrace. We have the price tags all mixed up, so that the cheap things have a high price on them, and the really precious things are priced low. And we let ourselves be taken in by it. What a costly mistake.

Conscientious citizens accept the responsibility of studying issues, and view candidates with an eye toward casting votes for people and issues that give high priority to feeding the hungry and housing the homeless.

We can give. Our government's failure to fund adequately for the poor does not relieve us of our own personal responsibility to help where and when we can. My neglect of the woman's pleas at University Village brought discomfort to me, but I would be sorry if it hadn't.

It is not easy to wed compassion and wisdom. There have been times when I have been "taken"—but as a rule, it is better to err on the side of mercy than to become indifferent and uncaring.

> *Not what we give, but what we share,*
> *For the gift without the giver is bare,*
> *Who gives himself with his alms, feeds three,*
> *Himself, his hungering neighbor and me.*
>
> —*James Russell Lowell*

Meaning of Success

P EOPLE WORSHIP SUCCESS because from our earliest hours we are encouraged to be successful. But we are not always certain just what success is and what we have to do to attain it.

In modern America, two questions are usually asked: How much is a person worth? (meaning how much money does the person have) and What has he or she done to get it? In other words, we have just two yardsticks for a successful life: accumulation and achievement.

When we resort to the vernacular and assert that someone is successful, we do not mean the person has developed a fine, helpful personality. When it is announced that someone has married well, it does not imply marriage to a person of sterling character or aspiring hopes. It means marrying into a relationship where there is financial stability or social status, or both.

There is nothing intrinsically wrong with affluence or social status. They usually indicate hard work and circumspect lives. However, history has proven again and again that we cannot appraise the value of success in monetary terms or social prestige.

In the nineteenth century, Europe produced two artists who had almost identical names. Millais, an English portrait painter, was the vogue in court circles of his day. He mingled with people of wealth, and had the knack of painting nobility as nobility loved to be painted. At the height of his career he had an income of thirty thousand pounds per year.

Millet, the great Flemish artist, was the Englishman's contemporary. Millet died from a disease brought on by malnutrition caused by his poverty. Although a pauper at his death, Millet left to the world the two immortal canvases, *The Angelus* and *The Man with a Hoe*.

People from all walks of life have stated what they conceived to be necessary tangibles and intangibles in a successful life. Their ideas are worth pondering.

The late Dr. William Menninger suggested six qualities that are essential to success: sincerity, personal integrity, humility, courtesy, wisdom, and charity.

An unknown author writes that people are successful who have lived well; laughed often and loved much; gained the respect of intelligent men and women and the love of children; who have filled their niche and accomplished their tasks; who leave the world better than they found it— whether by an improved poppy, a perfect poem, or a rescued soul; who have never lacked appreciation of the earth's beauty or failed to express it.

Elbert Hubbard, American writer and editor, described a successful person as one who has tried, not cried; who has worked, not dodged; who has shouldered responsibility, not evaded it; who has got under the burden, instead of standing off, looking on and giving advice.

William Ellery Channing, organizer of the American Unitarian Association in 1825, was one of life's choice spirits. "There is no market," he said, "for wet blankets."

My father's formal education was limited, but the wisdom he shared with his growing family shall never be forgotten. It was during my college days that he placed in my hand a card containing six suggestions for success. I believe these ideas were not original with him, but he incorporated them in his life and demonstrated their validity. To be successful, one has to be able to:

- Do one's duty even when one is not watched.
- Keep at the job until it is finished.
- Make use of criticism without letting it whip you.
- Bear injustice without retaliating.
- See the evil in the world, yet be ready to believe the best about others.

Finally,

> *Trust not each accusing tongue*
> *As most weak persons do;*
> *But still believe that story wrong*
> *That ought not to be true.*

❧

Saintly Skeptics

OME TIME AGO, I visited with a church member who told me that, although her husband never attended church services with her and professed no faith of his own, he is, she said, one of the finest, kindest, most upright, and caring persons she has ever known.

I know such people, and you do too—admirable men and women, splendid citizens, their moral integrity unimpeachable, loyal supporters of real values and tireless helpers of others—who make no commitment to any religious body.

We who believe in organized religion, and affirm that faith is maintained and propagated by communal structures, encourage all to share in the life of a religious institution. We lament the absence of those who make no commitment, but we are not judgmental of them. We rejoice in the good they do and profit by wise insights they may share.

There are two, among many, "non-believers" who have influenced my thinking and the thinking of millions of others. They are Albert Camus (1913-1960) and Henry L. Mencken (1881-1956).

It is not surprising that students preparing for the ministry today read the work of Albert Camus, a French scholar and writer. Though he was an avowed unbeliever, seminary students seem to find kinship and affinity with him.

Camus asked, in terms urgent for our generation, the really big questions. He set his face against three of the evils of our time: apathy, irresponsibility, and tyranny, and responded to the call of duty, honor, and love. He never lost sight of people in his concern for causes. He believed that greatness is not in being strong, but in the right use of strength.

Searching for it, longing for it, he could not discover any ultimate meaning in life, yet he lived heroically, and nobly served the causes he believed to be just, true, and right.

In his books, there is an honest and deep grappling with the religious dimensions of existence. Only God knows, but I suggest that Albert Camus, an avowed unbeliever, may have been closer to the state of grace than many who are conventionally religious.

H. L. Mencken is another example of grace at work in one who made light of traditional religion. He was an author, critic, social historian, and longtime editor of the *Baltimore Sun.* He seemed to pride himself in cynicism and agnosticism.

To the general public, Mencken was notorious for his acid criticisms and his roaring invective, but to his intimates, he was known as incomparably considerate and kind.

Everywhere Mencken went, he seemed to touch the humble, needy, and lonely with unusual caring and empathy. He invested two afternoons each week calling on the sick and lonely in hospitals. Doctors and nurses trooped after him as he visited hospital rooms, watching him distribute armloads of books, and listening to his words of cheer, funny quips, and clownish, farcical lectures on medical topics.

What do you make of a man like Mencken? Religiously, he was unorthodox, to say the least, and irreverent at worst. But in behavior he sometimes came close to saintliness. If godliness means reaching beyond conventional religious doctrines to perform the god-like deed, H. L. Mencken had a depth of godliness that would put many conventionally religious people to shame.

God is in no way obligated to live only where people look for Him, God often appears where we least expect to find Him, and in the most unlikely people. The faithful expect God to do the unexpected, and wise men know now, as they knew long ago, to look for the Eternal where others would scarcely guess His presence.

❧

Make it Fizz

BE GLAD YOU Are Not Beautiful" was the title of a magazine article I read many years ago. It was written by James F. Bender, who was then the director of the National Institute of Human Relations. The title caught my eye and I read the article immediately, for it offered a word of hope!

Mr. Bender made some interesting observations. He said that youngsters blessed with attractive physical features consistently do worse in school. "Parents," he wrote, "need to demand more of them to counteract the tendency to trust in their good looks."

Attractive young people, he continued, are less likely to be successful in their jobs; and average-looking people have a better chance of a happy marriage.

He pointed out that our most conspicuously handsome presidents—Warren G. Harding, James Buchanan, Franklin Pierce, and Chester A. Arthur—are all rated by historians as among our most ineffectual, least distinguished national leaders. The author also suggested that plain-looking people have a better chance of aging attractively.

These were interesting observations. I have often pondered their validity. William Osler, the famed medical doctor and teacher, counseled his students to marry a girl with freckles, for she will be inclined to be more amiable; and Benjamin Franklin advised a friend to marry a homely girl because such a woman would give more thought to being a good wife. (I can hear this proposal now—"I want to marry you, dear, because you are so homely"). I wouldn't recommend that today!

Some of the conclusions proposed are open to question. But there may be some truth in them. I suppose it would be an advantage to be handsome or pretty. You could get attention without trying too hard. But after the first five minutes, you're on your own.

There are risks involved in being physically attractive and endowed with other gifts. I have seen particularly well-muscled young men at the beach whose struts gave evidence that their muscles had gone to their heads, bringing undue pride.

People often break at the point of their excellence. For instance, a speaker might rely on a beautiful voice, a well-stocked vocabulary, glibness of speech, or an attractive platform presence instead of the more important matters: ideas, toil, and fidelity to the truth.

Ralph Waldo Emerson relates a fable about a quarrel between a mountain and a squirrel. The mountain derided the squirrel because of its size, to which the squirrel replied, "I think it's no disgrace to occupy my place. If I am not as large as you, you are not as small as I, and not half so spry. Talents differ. If I cannot carry forests on my back neither can you crack a nut."

Dr. Harry Emerson Fosdick was one of the greatest ministers of this century. His ministry reached millions. Union Seminary is across the street from Riverside Church. One day, a professor at Union gave wise counsel to his ministerial students. Pointing to Riverside Church, he said, "Don't let that incredibly brilliant man destroy your ministry. We can't all be Fosdicks. You give what you have to give. Angels can do no more."

Gipsy Smith, a great English evangelist (1860-1947), told of a young minister who came to him and asked for help in finding a job. One of the first questions Gipsy Smith asked was, "Can you preach?" The young man said, with humility, "I guess I wouldn't set the Thames on fire." "No," Mr. Smith said, "I suppose not. But if I threw you in, could it make it fizz?"

Most of us will not set the world afire, but we can make a little fizz at the place where our lives are lived. Great ability is important. But God is not so much interested in our ability as in our availability—the will to do what we can. We are foolish not to be what we can be, for all have different gifts, and the world needs the particular gift that each individual can offer.

We may long to accomplish great and noble tasks. But it is possible to do the humble, mundane tasks of every day as though they were great and noble. The world is moved toward truth, justice, and love—not only by the mighty shoves of its great heroes, but also by the aggregate of the tiny pushes of each conscientious, honest individual.

❦

Generosity's Reward

CHURCHES, SYNAGOGUES, YMCAs and YWCAs, United Way, and a host of other service-oriented institutions are gearing up for their annual fundraising drives, seeking financial pledges to meet the responsibilities and opportunities of the coming year. Money translates into helpfulness in meeting a multitude of human needs.

I have never cared for the terms "filthy lucre" or "petty cash." Money, when devoted to meeting human problems in helpful ways, is never filthy, and I have never seen any "petty cash." However, I have heard of some petty purposes for which some cash has been used.

We are all aware that money talks, although it seems hardly on speaking terms with some people, and it keeps saying "good-bye" to others. Yet it does speak a language that describes the one who possesses it.

Money in itself is neither good nor evil, but it can become a blessing or a curse, according to the way it is handled, as expressed in these lines of an unknown author:

> *Dug from the mountainside, washed from the glen,*

Servant am I or master of men.
Steal me, I curse you,
Earn me, I bless you;
Grasp me and hoard me, a fiend shall possess you,
Live for me, die for me,
Covet me, take me
Angel or devil, I am what you make me.

The late Dr. Karl Menninger lamented that many conscientious parents who are careful about the education of their children permit them to grow up untrained in the art of giving.

"Perhaps," he wrote, "the child's stability in the years ahead, his maturity and usefulness in society, is conditioned more by this practice than any other one thing. Money giving is a very good criterion of mental health. Generous people are rarely mentally ill people. I don't know how many hundreds of patients are now asloop in the graveyard, leaving behind them far more money than their children could amicably divide, causing endless trouble, worry, and, oftentimes, injury."

Twenty-two years ago a friend of mine, Hugh Brady, gave me a card which remains today under the glass that covers my desk. It reads: "There are no luggage racks on a hearse."

Brady took those words seriously and gave thousands of dollars for scholarships for young men attending Yale University. At the time of his death and memorial service, hundreds of men and women came to St. Mark's Cathedral testifying to their gratitude for his generosity.

Privilege humbly possessed and unselfishly dedicated,

perchance sacrificially denounced, is one of the noblest of human responses.

Dr. Albert Schweitzer demonstrated as clearly as any how to receive, live with, and wisely distribute what was his. Born into privilege, he saw its perils, and determined at an early age to seek his happiness and usefulness by limiting his desires rather than trying to satisfy them.

He did not see the money he had as his own, but as public money, a fund entrusted to him for proper disbursement. His living standards were not so austere as to be intimidating to those around him who sought some of life's comforts, but he pressed his claim, in whatever company, that those who are spared personal pain and poverty are called to help by sacrificing some of their own comfort to bring comfort to others.

His lifestyle was simple, his wardrobe unpretentious. He was often pictured in his dark rumpled suit and black string tie. While he was a guest at the home of Bishop Gerald Kennedy in California, he asked the eminent clergyman how many ties he had. "I'm not sure," replied Kennedy, "I have not counted them, but I suppose I have at least thirty-two."

"What!" responded Schweitzer. "Thirty-two ties and only one neck?" While Schweitzer's way of life may seem extreme to some, his selfless manner is a challenge to the possessive inclinations that plague the human spirit and deny support to many worthy causes today.

It is common to think of a philanthropist as someone who donates large sums of money. The word is derived from two Greek words, *philos* which means "loving" and *anthropos* which means "man." The two together mean "loving man or woman." This means that everyone who gives in love is a philanthropist, regardless of the amount given.

We all wish we could give more to the causes we support, and we rejoice in those who make substantial contributions to worthy causes. But the large gifts given by others do not release anyone from the responsibility of doing what can be done. The important thing is to express compassion and caring in some tangible way in response to the particular need before us.

An old Quaker, passing along the street, saw a cartman's horse fall dead. It was a serious loss, for the horse was the man's livelihood. The bystanders shook their heads and clucked sympathetically. The Quaker took off his broad-brimmed hat, placed a bank note in it and said, "Friends, I am sorry for this man ten dollars worth. How sorry are you?"

> *It's not what we'd do with a million*
> *If riches should e'er be our lot,*
> *But what are we doing at present*
> *With the dollar and quarter we've got?*

❧

NOVEMBER

Why Me?

REMEMBER SEEING A pamphlet by the United States Army when a crisis abroad necessitated calling thousands of reservists to active duty. This was an unexpected disruption of schedule for our American reservists. More than one man surveying the shambles of his plans was aware that others in the reserves were not called. So while they responded to their country's call they did so with the question, "Why me?" on their lips.

It was because so many men were asking the question that the Defense Department prepared a pamphlet titled, *Why Me?* In it, the Army explained the rationale behind this call to active duty. The pamphlet's title intrigued me as a subject of universal interest. For this is not just a question confined to those men whose prospects were fractured by a call to military service. It is a question that we all have asked when faced with disappointment in one form or another.

Often we feel we are the holders of some monogrammed misfortune, and have a personal propensity for trouble. We look at other human beings and marvel that they do not seem to be bothered with the burdens that plague us. We express our resentment in a host of characteristic reactions: "Well, wouldn't you know this would happen to me?" ... "Some people get all the breaks." ... "What have I done to deserve this?" ... all variations of the same "Why me?" theme.

Yet, in fairness, if we ask the "Why me?" question in regard to our burdens, we should also ask it in regard to our blessings. For this is the other side of the coin. If we complain about what seems to be undeserved hardship, should we not also rejoice in undeserved happiness? For some reason, this is immeasurably harder to do.

We take for granted one hundred days of perfect health, and then grumble about one day of aches and pains. We return home safely for a hundred trips without a song of gratitude, but in the one where we encounter problems or delays, we cry out in despair. We drive the freeway hundreds of times on schedule, but on the occasion when we suffer a flat tire or engine trouble, we ask, "Why me?" We casually accept when our family is together for the holidays, but if it is scattered or separated, we dwell on our loneliness. How often do we say, "Why me?" as we count our blessings? Do we wonder what we have done to deserve so many good things?

Every once in a while, we do touch shoulders with someone, in person or through literature, who does. Gilbert K. Chesterton, the great English essayist, was one who did. He had a marvelous sense of humor and a great deal of common sense. Throughout all of his writings he gives evidence of his deep appreciation for the commonplace blessings which so many overlook.

It was not that his life was unusually smooth or sunlit.

One of the disappointments of the Chestertons was that they never had children of their own. One of his biographers comments, "What was unusual with both Gilbert and Frances Chesterton was the fact that they never allowed their disappointment in the matter of children to make them sour or jealous of others who were experiencing the joy they had missed."

In their lives you will find nothing of self-pity or sorrow over what they lacked, but rather a kind of rollicking rejoicing over all that they had. Chesterton wrote, "You say grace before meals. All right. But I say grace before the concert and the opera, and grace before the play and pantomime, and grace before I open a book, and grace before sketching, painting, and swimming, fencing, boxing, walking, playing, dancing, and grace before I dip the pen in the ink."

Chesterton kept asking, "Why me?" to quite a different tune from the doleful dirge which generally accompanies the question.

There are many times in life when we do have both the occasion and the opportunity to ask "Why me?" in response to life's bountiful blessings. The Thanksgiving season is but one.

❧

Living Daily

RINCIPAL L. P. Jacks, the noted English philosopher, described every human heart as an arena where a hero and a coward wage a continuous conflict for the mastery of each personality. Upon the outcome of the struggle between the hero and the coward hinges our self-respect, our usefulness, and our happiness.

It is no sham battle. Because the struggle is both universal and life-long, with first one side of us and then the other victor, there are very few perfect heroes and heroines, and very few absolute cowards. Successful living pivots on courage.

Courage is the ability to act effectively in the face of danger or difficulty. It involves both purpose and knowledge of danger. The deepest courage is revealed when a person looks straight at danger or hardship and is not turned aside by it.

Those who do a dangerous thing in response to a dare or in order to prove that they are not afraid are reckless and foolhardy rather than courageous. A courageous person takes chances for the sake of an important cause. Courage is often confused with the absence of fear. But there is no such thing as courage without fear.

We read of courageous people who return to burning houses in an effort to save a life or leap into churning waters to save someone from drowning. Most of us have few opportunities, if any, to demonstrate courage or cowardice in such dramatic ways. It is usually in some less spectacular manner that courage or cowardice comes to the fore.

Many people need courage to meet the challenge of routine—the drudgery of life. It is often easier to "mount up with wings like eagles" than it is to "walk and not faint." Life can become very daily, and it is not easy to glorify the grind. The test of a man's or woman's courage is the way he or she faces and deals with sameness.

Anyone can die, but it often takes greater courage just to live. It takes courage for a teacher or student to study day in and day out, for a secretary to see romance in typing weeks on end. Cooking meals and washing dishes each day cannot easily be called an exhilarating exercise. And we can give a chuckle at the cartoon of a mother standing in a toy-strewn room, trying to separate two scrapping children while dinner boils over on the stove, lifting her head to heaven as she cries, "Sometimes I wish that I had loved and lost."

People who tackle life's relentless chores with bravery make a constructive contribution to their own lives and to the lives of those about them.

Neither fame, nor place, nor wealth can safeguard us from our share of dreams that don't come true or the death of those we love.

Life's real heroes and heroines are not the entertainers on stage and screen, or the athletes who dazzle crowds with their skills. Rather, they are those who have taken life's losses in stride. They prevail. They rest their faith in the God of the psalmist: "The Lord is my light and my salvation; whom shall I fear? The Lord is the strength of my life; of whom shall I be afraid?"

Giving What's Yours to Give

ONAH KALB AND David Wiscott, authors of the book, *What Every Kid Should Know*, point out that youngsters are exposed in school to many different subjects and fields of learning, all of which require varying skills. That's good.

The trouble comes when a school expects a youngster to be great in all of them. And individual teachers have a way of thinking that every student in the class ought to be good in that particular subject. That's ridiculous.

It would be humorous if it didn't make so many students feel so inadequate. Nobody is good at everything, but adults often expect this of kids, making them feel like failures. It is important to recognize that no adult expects another adult to be good at everything.

Why place that burden on youngsters?

Centuries ago, Confucius spoke words that deserve to be heard in every century: "Seek not every quality in one individual." Will Rogers said it for our generation: "We are all ignorant, only in different ways, and no one is as ignorant as an educated man outside his own field."

Even the great figures of history had their imperfections. William Butler Yeats and George Bernard Shaw were poor spellers. Ben Franklin, Pablo Picasso, and Carl Jung had trouble with mathematics. One of Albert Einstein's teachers called him mentally slow, and Isaac Watts was called dull and inept.

But God has a purpose for each individual, and no gift of mind or spirit is so small or useless that it cannot be turned to a constructive end. Each individual has a unique gift to offer that distinguishes him or her from all others.

We do not have to be the brightest member of a class in order to make a significant contribution to the school. I remember a classmate at college who once said to me, "Dale, I'm in the bottom third of our class. I help make the top two-thirds possible. But," he continued jokingly, "no one of us is worthless. Even the worst of us can serve as horrible examples."

But my classmate was not without his skills. He had a genius for friendship. He never met a stranger or an unimportant person. He was so outgoing he could lead a parade and greet every individual along the way.

He was not only a marvelous greeter, but an empathetic listener. He gave undistracted attention and showed genuine interest in even casual conversation. He heard others out without putting anyone down. Far from being a horrible example, he was a beautiful example for us all. In spite of what he felt was an average mind, he knew how to live his life and make the most of what he had.

In using wisely and lovingly the skills and learning they have, those who have not had the privilege and opportunity for a great amount of formal schooling can make life brighter for themselves and those around them.

Larry Holmes, the former heavyweight boxing champion, gave millions of dollars to his little home community in Pennsylvania to improve the quality of life for residents. When quizzed about his education, Holmes meekly replied, "I have a fourth-grade education in the public-school system, but a Ph.D. in common sense."

I have remembered through the years the saving grace that came to me in college from a statement by Oliver Wendell Holmes, that one of the great reliefs of life is to discover our own mediocrity. But this discovery—this realization that we do not possess all wisdom and every skill— is no excuse for not making whatever contribution we can.

Even the smallest hair casts a shadow. Unless we do the work for which we were created, our work is never done.

Jesus believed there were extraordinary powers that could be expressed through ordinary people, and he demonstrated this belief in his work with his disciples. It is doubtful if a more unpromising company could have been found in all Palestine than the group of humble men who followed Jesus, but they turned the world upside down, and carried the message of love and redemption to the rim of civilization.

When I was in junior high school, a teacher required each student to memorize simple lines from an unknown author. I have been happy to carry it with me all these years, and pass it on to you:

> *If you can't be a pine on the top of a hill*
> *Be a scrub in the valley, but be*
> *The best little scrub on the side of the hill.*
> *Be a bush if you can't be a tree.*

If you can't be a bush, be a bit of the grass
And some highway happier make.
If you can't be a muskie, then just be a bass
But the liveliest bass in the lake.

We can't all be captains, we've got to be crew.
There's something for all of us here.
There's big work to do and there's lesser to do
And the thing we must do is the near.

If you can't be a highway, then just be a trail.
If you can't be the sun, be a star.
It isn't by size that you win or you fail.
Be the best of whatever you are.

❧

A Lack of Love

ILLIAM JAMES, THE Harvard philosopher, and Bertrand Russell, the British humanist, were often far apart in the philosophies that governed their lives, but on one point they were in total agreement.

Each affirmed that the deepest need of the human spirit is to be loved and accepted. Their conclusions are substantiated by the whole of human experience. Rejection, at the opposite end of the pole, is the most desolate and demoralizing of the human conditions.

Our bodies can absorb a lot of punishment—unrelieved thirst, unwise diets, sleepless nights, and years of back-breaking toil. Our minds are no less durable. We can work without let-up for days. We can stretch to receive, store, and recall more information and adjust to new truth. We can grapple gamely with paradox and contradiction. But rejection is the hardest blow of all to bear. It can erase a smile, stoop shoulders, buckle the knees, snap the mind, and break the heart.

Rejection contributes to feelings of self-negation and a sense of worthlessness. Talents that might have been remain either unborn or unused. Fear of rejection is at the root of virtually all conformity. Rather than risk rejection, some people compromise their moral, cultural, and intellectual standards. Some who drink or use drugs would prefer not to, but they fear to refrain lest they be rejected. Some feel obligated to approve of books for which they have no sympathy because to disapprove would mean rejection by others.

We are gregarious creatures, more in our minds than in our bodies. We don't mind going alone for a walk, but we hate to stand alone in our convictions. The longing not to be nothing is one of the sharpest hungers a human can know. Many of the disturbances that occur in prisons are traceable to feelings of rejection. Men and women have rioted for names instead of numbers. To address another by name is to affirm that person's dignity and identity.

Rejection often touches off a chain reaction that starts with self-pity, moves to sour grapes (who wanted to belong to that group anyway?), goes on to bitterness, and finally hardens into thoughts of vengeance.

Rejection often leaves a sad wake. I think, as I write, of the boy who began life with all of the classic handicaps: a domineering mother, a deserting father, and a low estimate of his own self-worth. Bereft of affection, acceptance, love, and disciplined training, that youngster became increasingly ugly and unlovable. The school psychologist described him at thirteen as not knowing the meaning of the words "love" and "acceptance." The girls rejected him, the boys fought him, and despite a high IQ, he failed. He quit school and joined the military.

The Marines ridiculed him and he was discharged as undesirable for resisting authority. Without friends, and feeling rejected and alone, he left for a foreign country. He had no talent, skill, or self-regard. He couldn't even qualify for a driver's license, but he did convince a foreign girl to marry him. He brought her to the United States, and she bore him two children before she developed the same contempt for him that others had.

Her rejection drove him deeper into despair. The night she rejected him for the last time he tried to find footing at a new job. And it was there, the next morning, on the sixth floor of the place of his new employment, on November 22, 1963, that Lee Harvey Oswald pulled the trigger, releasing the bullet that killed President John F. Kennedy.

Perhaps history would be different if somewhere in Oswald's life there had been even one person who, although knowing his failings, could still have brought him enough love to rescue him from total rejection. How different it might have been if someone could have assured him of the steadfast love and acceptance of his Creator.

The Bible teaches in countless ways that God's love is unalterable and unconditional. Acceptance by God is not something to be hoped for, or worked for. It is given. This is the Good News of the Bible. God loves and accepts us not because we are good or bad, male or female, white, black, red, or yellow, Christian, Buddhist, Jewish, or Atheist, educated or uneducated, talented or inept, American, Chinese, Japanese, Russian, or Italian, but because we are His children.

It is the kind of love and acceptance that humans are called to reveal to one another. It does not entail approval of everything that is done anymore than God approves of everything we do, but love and acceptance are always present. When humans cease to point the finger of judgment and begin to extend the hand of friendship and the arms of love, we will be drawn closer to one another, and thus closer to the God who created us all.

Gratitude

IME GOES BY so quickly, and one season merges so rapidly into the next that it hardly seems possible the holidays are here again.

> The Christmas lights along the street
> The tinsel in the stores we enter
> The carols from the record shops
> The Santas in the shopping center
> The children lobbying for toys
> Without which life won't be worth living
> All make us conscious of the fact
> That it won't be long 'til Thanksgiving.

It is possible that in anticipating and getting ready for Christmas, we can almost crowd out Thanksgiving Day and make of it a lesser celebration. But it is very important that we do not leap-frog Thanksgiving.

"Gratitude," said Martin Luther, "is the basic Christian attitude."

When G. K. Chesterton wrote his autobiography close to the end of his long and useful life, he challenged himself to define in one simple sentence the most important lesson he had learned. He concluded that the critical thing in life was whether he took things for granted or received them with gratitude.

Gratitude always works. We can do our best only when we have thankful hearts.

The ungrateful have never done lovely things, but those who are grateful add beauty to the world.

Thanksgiving Day was born in the cradle of adversity. It was on August 20, 1620, that our Pilgrim fathers and mothers began their hazardous journey from foreign shores. In a day when travel has become so commonplace, it is difficult for us to imagine the discomforts of two months on the tiny, storm-tossed Mayflower.

They arrived when the autumn colors were already on the trees. Ahead of them was a winter in which nearly half their number was to die from the rigors of climate and the ravages of disease. When spring finally came, the captain of the returning Mayflower offered free passage to anyone who wished to return, but not a single person sought passage.

If the pilgrims had computed their income, Plymouth would have been a wailing wall instead of a festival. But these hardy souls had faith that out of their struggles and hardships would come a better world, so in the fall of 1621 a day of feasting was called.

True, thanksgiving has never depended on outward circumstance. The Apostle Paul lived a hounded life, but his epistles are punctuated by fountains of praise. In his first letter to the Thessalonians he wrote, "In everything give thanks, for this is the will of God in Jesus Christ concerning you."

He did not say we should be thankful for everything. We would be less than sane if we glorified illnesses, accidents, privations, and death. No, he did not say *for* everything, but *in* everything—that is, in every circumstance, maintain a thankful spirit.

This, of course, is not easy. We all share the hope of the woman who said, "It would be wonderful sometime to receive a blessing that wasn't in disguise."

We are not always free to choose what will happen to us, but we are free to choose what our response will be, and we have at least two alternatives. We can respond angrily with resentment, "Why did *this* have to happen?" Or we can sift through what has happened and say, "What can we find here to be thankful for?" Our attitude determines whether we are victim or victor.

It is the grace of gratitude that gradually overtakes and overcomes grief. Dr. John Claypool, one of America's great ministers, writes about the evolution of his emotions following the death of a daughter. He writes first about the anger and despair he knew, then he writes:

> We can understand something as a gift and handle it with gratitude, a perspective Biblical religion puts around all of life. And I am here to testify that this is the only way down from the Mountain of Loss. I do not mean to say that such a perspective makes things easy, for it does not. But at least it makes things bearable when I remember that Laura was a gift, pure and simple, something I neither earned nor deserved nor had a right to.
>
> And when I remember that the appropriate response

to a gift, even when it is taken away, is gratitude, then I am better able to try to thank God that I was ever given her in the first place.

An old gospel song encourages us to "Count your many blessings; Name them one by one; And it will surprise you what the Lord has done." I'm sure it is not a great hymn, but I'm equally sure it is sound philosophy for the living of each day. When we take the time to count our blessings, we are surprised to see how many there actually are.

DECEMBER

To See Greatness before it Blooms

NE SPRING DAY, sometime before the Civil War, a young man came to the door of Worthy Taylor's farmhouse in Portage County, Ohio, asking for work. Although Taylor knew nothing about the fellow, he decided to take a chance on him and gave him a job doing general farm labor.

Jim cut stove wood, brought the cows in from pasture, and helped with the milking and haying. He slept in the haymow. As the summer wore on, Jim fell in love with Taylor's daughter. But Worthy Taylor refused to let Jim marry his daughter, pointing out that Jim was without money, without a name that commanded respect, and without prospects of ever making a name for himself or a decent living.

So Jim packed his few possessions and left the farm.

Thirty-five years passed, and the farmer Taylor prospered. He needed to tear down his barn and build a new and much bigger barn. It was then that he discovered that Jim had carved his name—"James A. Garfield"—on one of the haymow rafters. In those thirty-five years, Jim had made a name that commanded respect for himself.

About that time, President Garfield was walking down a street in Washington, D.C., with a friend when the two saw a newsboy approaching them. Garfield saluted the youngster as they passed.

His friend asked why he had saluted. "You never know," replied the president, "what is buttoned up in one of those jackets."

One of the marks of greatness is the ability to be able to see potential greatness in others. But it is amazing that some otherwise sensible people have a way of seeing only the negative aspects in every situation. Like vultures, they fly over much that is good and beautiful, looking for something that is dead. They always see the problem and not the promise.

When Walter Scott began his boyish attempts to write by jotting down a few lines of poetry, his father did his best to discourage him. "These improfitable flights of your fancy will lead you nowhere," he warned.

High-school teachers considered Honoré de Balzac stupid and actually made fun of him to his face. "This fat little fellow goes around in a state of intellectual coma," one of them said.

A grandfather once poured ten shillings into the cupped hands of his grandson, who had just written a eulogy to his grandmother. "This is the first money you have ever earned for the writing of poetry," said the grandfather, "and you can be very sure it will be the last." The boy who received those coins was Alfred, Lord Tennyson.

Some years ago, the French people voted for who they considered to be the outstanding Frenchman of all time. Who was selected? Napoleon? No. It was Louis Pasteur.

Yet when Pasteur was a schoolboy, one teacher described him as, "the meekest, smallest, least promising boy in the class."

Robert Browning traced much of his success as a writer to the encouragement he received from his father when he was a boy.

Nothing lifts us up and sets us moving toward greater accomplishments more than the simple word or gesture of appreciation for that which we have already done. I don't think we should make any apology for declaring this need for ourselves. William James said, "The deepest principle of human nature is the craving to be loved and appreciated."

It is love that sees the possibilities in others. "Love is blind" is one of the many proverbs that is only partially true. Love is the only reality that really sees. Love calls into being what is hidden, but nonetheless, real. Goodness may be only in the embryonic stage, but love can bring it fully alive.

And there is goodness in everyone. It remains only to be discovered.

"I love you," wrote Roy Croft of his friend, "not only for what you are, but for what I am when I am with you. I love not only for what you have made of yourself, but for what you are making of me.

"I love you for the part of me which you bring out—for putting your hand into my heaped-up heart and passing over all the foolish, weak things that you can't help dimly seeing there, and for drawing out all the beautiful belongings that no one else had looked quite far enough to find…"

Jesus believed every person was potentially good, and his affirmation helped to bring that goodness alive.

Zaccheus, the crooked tax collector, became honest. Mary, the woman of the streets, sinned no more. Volatile, tempestuous, impulsive Peter became Peter, the rock, symbol of stability.

> *Love came down at Christmas*
> *Love all lovely, Love Divine;*
> *Love was born at Christmas,*
> *Stars and angels gave the sign.*
>
> *Love shall be our token,*
> *Love be yours, and Love be mine,*
> *Love to God and all men,*
> *Love for plea, and gift, and sign.*

—*Christina Rossetti*

The Gift of Touch

OD HAS GIVEN us many marvelous gifts, but none more wonderful than the gift of touch. Through the gift of touch, humans move toward the solidarity and closeness God ordained. Our deepest feelings are often expressed through touching experiences, being touched, or keeping in touch.

Despite what the best of science, instinct, and common sense tells us, many Americans cut down on the amount and quality of physical contact. After infancy, words replace touches; distance replaces closeness. Care is often taken to make sure that youngsters don't see their own parents touching each other affectionately. Many parents, who confuse the sexual touch with caring, restorative, or sympathetic touch are either afraid or ashamed to make physical contact with growing sons and daughters.

The need for physical closeness is ever present—and the neglect of it is regrettable, and often destructive. Touch plays a vital role in giving encouragement, expressing tenderness, and in showing emotional support.

Touch is a crucial aspect of all human relationships. However, except in moments of extreme crisis, we often forget how to ask for it—or to offer it.

Anne Davis, a contemporary writer, tells a poignant story of her childhood. She says the first time she ever spent the night with a friend, she was amazed when the little girl's mother came in and hugged and kissed her daughter goodnight. In Anne's family, this kind of overt affection had never been shown, but seeing it made her hunger for it deeply.

So, she said, the next night when she was back in her own home and it was time to be tucked into bed, she put her cheek up in a very prominent place, but nothing happened. Her mother simply went through her usual ritual of laying out clean clothes for the next school day. Anne cried herself to sleep that night and concluded that her mother must not love her as much as her friend's mother loved her daughter. That disappointment sank deep within her and festered for years.

It was not until she was an adult that she related this experience to her mother and asked why she had not shown more physical affection. At that point, her mother's eyes filled with tears and she said, "I didn't grow up in a home where that was done. Since my mother died when I was five, no one came to tuck me in and tell me goodnight.

"Also, there was no one who washed our clothes regularly, and I often had to go to school in a dirty dress, humiliated and embarrassed. I made up my mind that if I ever had any children of my own, the one thing they would always have would be clean clothes. This is the way I tried to show my affection." At that moment, there were two sets of eyes full of tears.

One of the fantasies that people have about love is that

if someone really cares about you, they will know automatically what you want and like, and that if they do not give you what you want, it is a sign that they do not love you. Such clairvoyance does not exist, but the truly loving person does know the need that all have for physical closeness, and exercise good judgment in the expressions of caring.

One of the dangers of our fear about child abuse is that children will be deprived of the legitimate expressions of physical closeness which assures our love and caring.

Others who need this assurance are the elderly. Few people touch the old, yet they need it, too. Long after sight, hearing, speech, and mental faculties have been lost, the sense of touch remains. Early in my ministry, while visiting in a nursing home, I sat by the bed of a ninety-two-year-old friend. Death was not far away. "I am not afraid," she said, "but I am lonesome. Will you hold my hand?" I did, until she breathed her last. Perhaps she voiced for all of us our deepest need—the gentle, caring touch.

A Time for Receiving

HRISTMAS IS A season for giving. It is also a time for receiving. Giving is readily recognized as a way of serving others, but learning to receive graciously is equally important.

Those who receive with genuine joy, enthusiasm, and deep appreciation contribute to the joy of the giver. We all know people who receive even our small favors so graciously that we wish we could have given more. Conversely, a lukewarm or qualified reception dims the joy of the donor.

We remember the little girl who received a pincushion from her grandmother, and wrote, expressing her gratitude, "Thank you, Grandma for the pincushion. I have always wanted a pincushion, but not very much."

When we receive gratefully from another, we enhance the person's sense of self-worth. Allowing others to give and being able to humbly receive smothers the strident clamor for self-insistence or personal domination. So, receiving humbly and gratefully becomes a gift—a giving. It changes one of the ugliest things in the world, patronage, into one of the richest gifts life can offer, friendships.

While in seminary, one of my friends gave me a new book. It was an expensive book, a gift beyond my deserving, and I knew it cost more than my friend could afford to spend. I responded by saying, "Ed, you should not have done this. You don't even have such a fine book for your own."

I could see he was crestfallen by my comments. After a moment of reflection, he told me, "When someone loves you and even sacrifices something of his own to give you a gift, don't, please don't, tell him he should not have done it. Don't make him feel he has exercised poor judgment or made a mistake in giving you a gift. Let him know you appreciate it very much. Don't kill his joy by being a poor receiver."

Warming to his lecture, he said one thing more, as I recall, "When someone gives you the gift of a compliment in words, don't disagree or minimize what he says, for words are gifts, too. Accept them gratefully, even though you think you don't deserve them."

An incident in the life of Jesus, recorded in Matthew, Mark, and John, reveals that both giving and receiving can be manifestations of love. A woman used precious ointment to anoint the feet of Jesus. The disciples criticized her for what they considered an unwise extravagance. "The ointment," they said, "could have been sold and the money given to the poor."

Jesus taught that the full life comes to those who give beyond what is required and are open to receive life's good gifts.

William Allen White, the renowned Kansas newspaperman, understood and applied this teaching. He was always ready to give more than expected and take less than he deserved, but lived his life with a receptive heart and mind.

He began each day with a spirit of expectation and anticipation of good things. He said, "I have never been bored an hour in my life. I get up each morning wondering what new, strange, glamorous thing is going to happen, and it happens at fairly regular intervals. Lady Luck has been good to me. I fancy she has been good to many. Only some people are dour, and when she gives them a come-hither with her eyes, they look down and turn away. But me—I give her the wink, and away we go."

Be ready to receive this Christmas, for receptivity is a gift. Learning to receive graciously is the greatest gift you can give to others—and to yourself.

❧

Miss McClure

FRIEND RECENTLY POSED two questions for a group of us who were talking about the past. He first asked if we remembered a favorite teacher, and then if we could recall our very first "heart throb" or love affair.

I found it easy to respond readily to those questions because my favorite teacher and first romance were tied up in the same person—Miss McClure—my second-grade teacher at Lawndale grade school in Kenmore, Ohio.

That she was twenty-seven and I was seven didn't make any difference at all. Why, shucks, I could catch up with her, and even if I couldn't, when she was ninety, I'd be seventy and people wouldn't notice all that much difference. Of course she would have to wait fifteen years or so until I was out of school before we could be married.

It was true that her boyfriend, who came to the school each evening to take her to her home, posed something of a threat, but I knew that as she came to know me better, he would pale by comparison.

I try now to understand why I loved Miss McClure so intensely. It isn't that I remember her as an exceptional teacher of mathematics or reading, although she would never permit anyone to be satisfied with shoddy work, and she continuously pressed all her students toward excellence.

My love for her had not only to do with how she often favored me by inviting me to remain after school to help her wash the blackboards, dust the erasers, tidy up the room, and gave me an apple from her overabundant supply.

It isn't because I remember her as a "good looker," for she wasn't all that pretty. I think the reason that my heart went out to her was because she was such a marvelous "overlooker." That is, she steadily refused to see my bad points even though they were many—dirty face, tousled hair, a nose that usually needed plumbing, and a behavior record that would not have won a good conduct medal. She just plain refused to see or concentrate on these and other negative qualities.

Instead, Miss McClure was sure that one day I would be the president of the United States or would preside at the Forum on the Day of Judgment. Because of that confidence in me, there were days when I washed and scrubbed my face and ears more than usual before starting for school, brushed my shoes and even combed my hair— that is, when I remembered.

Miss McClure was a teacher who knew how to affirm her students. She saw through each one in such a way as to enable her to see each one through. She was not blind to any students' inadequacies, but she chose to see beneath the soil to the seeds of promise.

When criticism did come, it came from her as summer

rain—gentle enough to nourish growth without destroying the roots of self-confidence. She always heard each class member out without putting anyone down. It was her philosophy to treat all people as if they were what they ought to be. In so doing, she believed she would help them to become what they were capable of becoming.

I'm sure there must have been other members of that second-grade class who were as much in love with Miss McClure as I was, for she was too wise a teacher to have favorites. Whatever her inner feelings might have been, she made each one of us feel extra-special.

Miss McClure, the grasses on your grave have been growing for many years, but ever fresh in my mind will be the memory of you. You were the first great "overlooker" I had ever met outside of my own family.

Happily, I have met many others since—other teachers and friends, my wife, and family members. They have been very kind to my virtues and a little blind to my faults. But Miss McClure, you were the first, and without knowing it, or perhaps even intending it, you gave me one of my first glimpses of what God is like. For God is the greatest overlooker of all—"I will blot out your sins, and remember your transgressions no more."

Like a Christmas Doughnut

HEN CHRISTMAS DRAWS near, I feel in my heart a great joy. But I must confess that, at the same time, there is in that same heart something that is sad. I can think of no other time in the year when I am aware of such a strange mingling of happiness and sadness.

This surely must be because Christmas touches our emotions at their most sensitive level—remembrances of one's own life at various stages of growth, or of friends and family members loved and long since departed. I suspect you understand what I am trying to say, for you, no doubt, have felt this same way.

I recall the Christmas of my childhood, with its beautifully decorated house and tree, the subtle scent of fruitcake, and the prevalence of candy and apples.

Best of all was that Christmas morning—early, of course—when I hurried down the stairs in the pre-dawn darkness and saw the football helmet that I, as a nine-year-old, had longed for.

But almost equaling that supreme moment was the fun that came earlier during Advent with all the traditional preparations going on. It was during those days that my brothers and sister and I delighted in watching our mother make doughnuts.

The process of doughnut making became more and more interesting as it neared completion. The last act was to take the sizzling doughnuts from the skillet, drop them into a pan of sugar and turn them over and over.

After they had cooled a bit, they were ready to go into a special doughnut jar, but I remember that quite a few of them never reached the jar! We thought they were much better when hot, and it always seemed a shame to us to have them lose any of their goodness by letting them cool. So Mother let us eat only as many as seemed wise before she put them in the jar.

She told us she had heard of one mother who put a lock on her cookie jar. A friend of hers said she thought that would be a clever idea, but she asked how she kept the children from finding the key. "Oh, that is easy," the woman said. "I just hide it under the soap."

Thinking back to the Christmas doughnuts, I remember that you can't touch a sugared doughnut without getting some sugar on your fingers. And it also leaves a trail of sweetness where ever it goes.

When I thought about this, it occurred to me that it would be a better world if somehow we could be like sugared doughnuts—leaving a trail of flavorful joy and fragrance behind us. Wouldn't it be great if everyone who had contact with us felt a little happier because their lives had touched ours? What a beautiful gift this would be to bring to a world in which there is so much bitterness, animosity, rancor, and violence.

We live in a world divided between people who think

they are right—and have seen recent evidences of this right in our own city. When some people walk into a room, they seem to light a candle.

Others blow it out. Some have a difficulty for every solution. They see only the hole in the doughnut.

Pope John XXXIII said, "I don't agree with the prophets of doom. They always talk as if the present, compared with the past, is getting worse. I see humankind entering a new era, and I see in this a divine plan. This plan, in the course of time and in and through what man does, pursues its own purposes, its own goals, and they are far, far beyond man's expectations."

Pope John was a realist. His faith in the future and his joy in the present had their roots in the response that is encouraged in the life and teachings of Jesus.

The dominating theme of the New Testament and the lives of Jesus and Paul is joy. Indeed, the very meaning of "gospel" is "good news."

The birth of Jesus was heralded by angels who proclaimed good tidings of great joy. His first public appearance was at a wedding where he made the guests happy. His last public appearance, according to the book of John, was around a campfire.

No words were more on his lips than "Be of good cheer," "Be not anxious," "Be not afraid," "Rejoice, and again I say, rejoice."

Jesus did not sadden life—he gladdened it. He did not believe he could eliminate gloom by adding to it. It's not likely he would have attracted and appealed to children as he did if he had been a dour, gloomy, and morose person.

Jesus' chief criticism of the scribes and the Pharisees

was that their interpretation of religion had become savorless—dull and plodding, mechanical and routine. There was no spontaneity, no joy.

The greatest foe of Christianity is not agnosticism or atheism, but men and women who, having entered the Christian life, have never had the Christian life enter them enough to help them to be the joyful, radiant, and attractive people they were intended to be.

Nothing impedes the expansion of Christianity like a dull, negative, lifeless representation of it. Nothing is more attractive and inviting than a Christian who makes his religion fun—one who serves the Lord with gladness.

Robert Louis Stevenson hardly knew a day of good health, but his unwillingness to be defeated by infirmity was always evident. Though sick, he was always singing, though cast down, he was not dismayed. His prayer is a motto for us all:

> *If I have faltered more or less in my*
> *great task of happiness*
> *If I have moved among my race and shown*
> *no glorious morning face*
> *If beams from happy human eyes*
> *have moved me not*
> *If morning skies, books, and my food and*
> *summer rain*
> *Knocked on my sullen heart in vain*
> *Lord, thy most pointed pleasure take*
> *And stab my spirit broad awake.*

Index

Index

Index

Acknowledgments

WITHOUT THE HELP of many generous and supportive people, this book, not to mention the past fifteen years of *Seattle Times* columns from which it came, would not have been possible. I would like to thank everyone who has played a part in making it a reality. Most especially I want to thank my wife, Leone, who has supported me in spirit for close to fifty years, as well as helping me to get these words on paper. Alex MacLeod, managing editor of *The Seattle Times* and my first editor, has been indispensible as a friend and advisor, as has everyone at the *Times*.

Finally, I thank Ruth Williamson-Kirkland, whose generous assistance and devotion have been an inspiration.

About the Author

THE REVEREND DOCTOR Dale Turner began his official ministry in Lansing, Michigan, in 1943 after graduating from Yale Divinity School. He had intended to become an athletic coach before his graduation from West Virginia Wesleyan College in 1940, and was able to combine this joy with that of youth minister in Lansing and Grand Rapids, Michigan.

In 1948 he accepted a call to become senior minister of Plymouth Congregational Church in Lawrence, Kansas. Here he served his community's spiritual needs for ten years as pastor, professor of religion at the University of Kansas, and chaplain of the Kansas football team. He was named "Man of the Year" in Lawrence in 1951.

He took the helm at University Congregational Church in Seattle, Washington in 1958. The compassionate and spirited length of his pastoral shadow cast far and wide throughout the University of Washington community, touching all parts of Seattle and beyond—from ministry in the slums of Japan to the pulpit of St. Giles Cathedral in Scotland. Since his retirement from the Seattle church in 1982, he has written a weekly column for the religion page of *The Seattle Times*.

Although Dr. Turner has received many honors, including the Outstanding Alumni Award of West Virginia Wesleyan, the Salvation Army "Others Award," Seattle's "First Citizen" award, the degree of doctor humanis causa from Seattle University, and the endowment of the Dale E. Turner Scholarship Fund at Yale Divinity School, he continues to believe himself to be no particular hero. Instead, he honors and nurtures the bravery in each person he meets and in every individual with whom he is acquainted.

Reverend Turner makes his home in Seattle with his multi-talented wife of forty-nine years, Leone. They have four sons, three daughters-in-law, six grandsons, and two granddaughters.

A Note on the Type

The text of this book was set in Caledonia, a typeface designed by the renowned designer and illustrator William A. Dwiggins (1880-1956) in 1939. Blending the elements of Scotch Roman and Bulmer typefaces, Caledonia has become one of the most widely used book types of all time, combining a sturdy simplicity with a lively calligraphic flare. This version of Caledonia (the Latin name for Scotland) was released by Linotype in the late 1980s as "New Caledonia." The text of this book was set electronically.

Printed and bound by RR Donnolley & Sons Co.
Crawfordsville, Indiana

Designed by Alex Lubertozzi